On the cover - A band of wild horse mounted Oglala Sioux warriors descends a hill. A young brave first learned to approach the enemy and take coup by touching him using the coup stick, hand or quirt. An act of bravery earned a feather. It was an honor to join a war party and go on a raid to take horses or enemy scalps. Scalping was learned from the French. A full eagle feather war bonnet, worn by a chief, exhibited much bravery.

To whom it may concern - The word squaw is not a guttural term. In actuality the word, squaw is an Algonquian term in the Narragansett Indian tongue and simply means an Indian's wife and was adopted into the white man's language. Some Native American women may think it to be demeaning, but it is not. I like to use it occasionally with no ill intent, because it is the word used back then for an Indian woman and is politically correct.

#1 Oglala Sioux Chief American Horse
Courtesy of Azusa Publishing, L.L.C.

THE LAKOTA SIOUX INDIANS,
A history of the Siouan people

ROBERT D. BOLEN, B.A.

Dedicated to
Doris Anne, Kerri Anne, James Eugene,
Jeromy David, Ryan Grady and Laura Brooke,
all of whom I hold dear.

#2. Aboriginal Wickiup
Courtesy of the American Library of Congress

5

ILLUSTRATIONS

Lakota Sioux Indians

Contents

Acknowledgements

My deepest thanks to Teresa, owner of Azusa Publishing, L.L.C., in Denver, Colorado for all of the wonderful iconic Indian post cards she has graciously allowed me to use in this text. The Curtis photos are superb. The pictures really make the book in my estimation. Her website and ad for gorgeous authentic Indian postcards is in the back of the book. I highly recommend the use of her fine web site.

I would like to thank the Library of Congress for the excellent ancient Wickiup photo and also thanks to the Smithsonian Institute for the picture of Washakie's village.

Kudos, to Bonnie Fitzpatrick (the Designer), for her formatting and graphic design. Bonnie does a great job!

I would like to thank Kathy from the Wal-Mart Photo staff and the team for their processing of pictures. Last, but not least, my sincerest thanks to Lightning Source (Ingram Publishing Company) for their fine job of printing this publication.

"Wopila tanka," many thanks in the Sioux Indian tongue!!

#3. Hidatsa Warriors
Courtesy of Azusa Publishing, L.L.C.

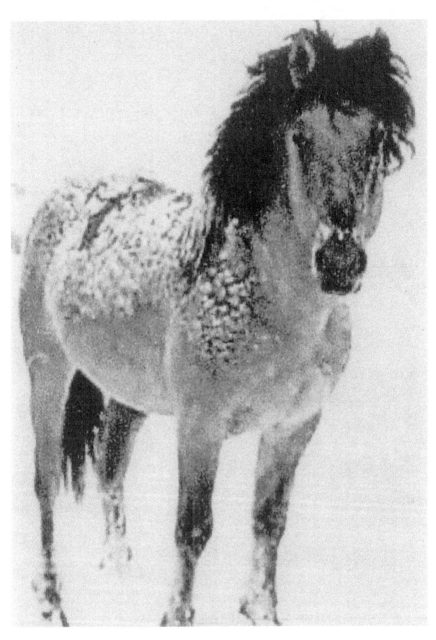

#4. Spanish Mustang
Courtesy of www.aaanativearts.com

FOREWORD

The great Sioux Nation once lodged in the Carolinas and ranged into Labrador. The Sioux are in the Siouan language family, spoken by many tribes in the Northern Plains and Great Lakes region. The Sioux Confederacy made up seven tribes and seven council fires of the great Lakota (Dakota) Nation. The Algonquian word for their tribe was *Nadowessioux* and from it came the word, Sioux Indian. Siouan speakers were a major language stock.

The divisions of the Sioux Confederacy were in four groupings, based on their subculture and dialect: the Santee, Teton, Yankton and the Yanktonai Sioux. The Lakota Nation was further divided into the Blackfoot Sioux, Brule, Minneconjou, Oglala, Sans Ark and Two Kettles. The Sioux were allied to the Arapaho and Cheyenne and mortal enemies of the Crow and Shoshoni Indians. Although the Sioux traded with the Mandan, they also fought them at times. The Sioux warriors fought nearly every Plains tribe.

John Smith encountered Siouan speaking peoples in Virginia in 1608. The Eastern Dakota Indians dwelled in pit houses in South Carolina and buried their dead in earthen mounds and were Woodland Indians, who migrated into the Upper Mississippi region in the 17th century on the Ohio, Minnesota and Wisconsin. The Sioux are a First Nation.

Militant Chippewa Indians traded early from English and French fur traders for the horse and firearms and drove the Sioux with their bows and arrows west into Dakota Territory in the 1700's. There, they hunted, fished and practiced some farming.

There were four bands of the Santee tribe. The name, Santee Sioux originated from the Siouan word "*Isáŋathi*," meaning "Knife." and dwelled east of the Dakotas, Minnesota and Iowa, known as Eastern Dakotas. The Western Dakota (Yankton) Sioux moved into Northern Minnesota and became crafters of fine pipes from Minnesota pipestone that they quarried. The Yankton Sioux (Middle Sioux) lodged in Iowa, southeastern South Dakota and southwestern Minnesota. Yankton and Yanktonai tribes dwelled in earthen lodges. In the eastern Dakotas, there were three bands of Yanktonai Sioux on the Upper Missouri River.

The Teton, Lakota or Western Sioux were the largest tribe. Lakota is translated, allied or many in one. They dwelt in the Black Hills of South Dakota, parts of Montana and Wyoming, were a warring tribe and fought over territory. The Sioux got the horse from the Cheyenne and Mandan Indians. The Sioux dominated central Canada to the Platte River, from the Minnesota River to the Yellowstone River, along with the Powder River country. They became Plains Indians, militant warriors and hunters of the buffalo. The Blackfeet, Comanche and Sioux Indians ruled the Plains.

The socio-political rule of the Siouan Indians was formed of a council, who decided important matters, such as the hunt, war and camp moves. Chieftains were chosen for character traits, like bravery in war, generosity and wisdom, as well as prowess on the hunt.

Societies were fraternal clans formed among the seven tribes of the Sioux Nation. Membership in the societies helped to elevate ones position in the tribe. Two major male societies were the *Akichita* society for the young men and the *Naca* society for the elders and political leaders. The *Naca Omniciye* society elected 7-10 men as chief men (*Wichasa Ithanchan*). These made and enforced decisions of the Nada. The Akichita trained warriors for combat, hunters and those who policed the community. Other smaller societies existed, such as the Elk, Kit-fox and Strong Heart, the society that Sitting Bull joined.

The Wichasa Ithanchan elected either two or four "Shirt Wearers" to speak for the society. They settled arguments among families and were young men from good families, who had taken leadership roles. One exception was Crazy Horse, who was common-born, yet chosen to be a Shirt wearer. The Sioux Indians became a powerful Indian nation to be reckoned with.

11

#5. American Buffalo
Author Photo

Chapter One
THE SIOUX NATION

Thousands of years ago, early man crossed the Bering Straits from Asia, the first humans on the American continent and followed the herds of bison-bison hunting for food and spread cross country from shore to shore.

The Sioux most probably migrated across the Bering Straits, Alaska and Canada into America (a First Nation) of North America. The Sioux were originally Woodland Indians inhabited subterranean earthen dwellings and were buried in earthwork mounds. They migrated from South Carolina, into the Upper Mississippi region of Iowa, Minnesota, Ohio and Wisconsin in the 17th century. Captain John Smith met the Eastern Sioux Indians near Jamestown, Virginia in 1608.

There were three divisions of the *Siouan* Confederacy based on their dialect and subculture, the *Santee* (Eastern Dakota) *Sioux*, the *Teton* (Lakota) or Western Sioux, and the *Nakota* (*Yankton* and *Yanktonai*) Sioux in seven tribes with seven great council fires in the Dakota or great Sioux Nation.

Dakota (allied) and Sioux are used synonymously. Santee came from the Siouan word *"Isáŋathi,"* or "Knife." The Santee dwelled east of the Dakotas in Minnesota and Iowa and had four bands; *Mdeakantonwon, Sisseton, Wakpekute and Wahpeton.*

The *Lakota* Sioux (prairie dwellers) were of the largest Plains tribe in America. The Teton were also called the Western Sioux, who dwelt in Montana, Nebraska, North Dakota, South Dakota and Wyoming and warred over territory. The Siouan speaking peoples inhabited Northern America

The Lakota Nation was divided into seven bands, the Blackfoot (Sioux), *Brule* (burnt thighs), *Hunkpapa* (end of the circle), *Minneconjou* (planters by the stream), *Oglala* (scatter their own), *Sans Arc* and Two Kettle (Boilings) bands. Sioux were hated by the Blackfeet, Crow, and Shoshoni.

Societies were fraternal clans formed among the seven tribes of the Sioux Nation. Two major clans were the *Akichita* society for braves and the *Naca* society for tribal elders.

The *Naca Omniciye* society elected seven men as chief-men (*Wichasa Ithanchan*), who enforced decisions of the Naca. Akichita trained warriors for combat, hunters, and to police the camps.

The *Wichasa Ithanchan* normally elected four young men, from good families as "Shirt Wearers," to speak for the society, who took leadership roles and settled arguments and more had duties. The shirt worn was probably a highly decorated (painted) deerskin war shirt. The *Wakichunza* (Pipe Holders) ranked slightly below the Shirt Wearers. The Pipe Holder Society orchestrated ceremonies, chose camp locations and supervised activities.

The Yankton (*Nakota*) or Middle Sioux lodged in Iowa, southeastern South Dakota and southwestern Minnesota. *Yankton* and *Yanktonai* tribes dwelled in earthen lodges and moved into northern Minnesota and were crafters of fine pipes of pipestone they quarried.

The Yankton divided into three bands: the Yankton, Upper Yankton and Lower Yankton. The Yanktonai Sioux dwelt along the Upper Missouri River, in the Eastern Dakota's.

The word Sioux came from the Chippewa term *Nadowessioux*, (snake or enemy), in the Algonquian dialect, and contained the word *Sioux*. The derivation is a corruption of its origin the way French trappers translated it. The Sioux people spoke the Siouan dialects, although they differed slightly. Next to the Algonquian, the Siouan language was the second largest linguistic family of American Indians and the most widespread.

Siouan Speakers

The Dakota-Assiniboine were formed of the Mdeakantonwon (Santee), Sisseton, Wahpekute, Wahpeton, Yankton, Yanktonai and Teton.

The Teton were made up of the Blackfoot (Sioux), Brule, Hunkpapa, Minneconjou, Oglala, Sans Arcs and Two Kettles. Assiniboine was an isolate.

The Djegiha language group contained the southern Sioux, Omaha-Ponca, the Kansa, Osage and Quapaw, Pahatsi, Santukhdhi and Utsehta.

The Chiwere group included the Iowa, Oto and Missouri Indians and also included the Winnebago and Mandan.

The Hidatsa group included the Hidatsa and Crow.

The Biloxi group included the Biloxi and the Ofo.

The Eastern Sioux division was made up of several confederacies of Siouan speakers not covered in this text.

#6. Offering to the Sun
Courtesy of Azusa Publishing Company, L.L.C.

The societal affiliation and brotherhoods were all important to the Sioux. They also had clans, secret societies based on medicine and powers. Small brotherhoods existed, such as the Elk, Kit-fox and Strong Heart societies. These societies helped to elevate ones position in the tribe. They dressed in colorful costumes and painted their bodies for festivities. The Kit- foxes wore fox skin necklaces and head-bands, adorned with kit-fox jawbones.

Dancing, Song and Storytelling were important to the Sioux, who did the Animal and Buffalo Dance, Calumet Dance, Ghost Dance, Grass Dance, Horse Dance, Medicine Dance, Scalp Dance, Victory Dance and War Dance.

The Sun Dance celebration was held in early summer annually on the Upper Heart River. It was the most important ceremony of the Sioux. The twelve day ritual involved dance, endurance, mutilation, self sacrifice, and unity. *Wiwanyag Wachipi* in the Sioux language meant looking at the sun.

Blackfoot Sioux, Hunkpapa, Minneconjou, Sans Arc Sioux and Cheyenne Indians attended the Sun Dance ceremonies. Arapaho Indians also observed the Sun Dance. The annual Sun Dance ranked above any ceremony during the year, a time when they worshipped their sacred sun god. They assembled, cut down and trimmed a cedar tree for a center pole for the dance.

The men first sought purification in a sweat lodge, before they lamented and prayed to the sun and said a pledge for the recovery of the sick and also offered songs to the sun. The Sun Dance was a religious ceremony for making a promise to the sun god. Warriors in danger in battle made a vow to the sun, that if their life was spared; they would dance the Sun Dance.

One type of self sacrifice was self torture performed by the warriors in the evening, who danced around the sun pole (center pole)

#7. Arapaho Indian Chief
Courtesy of Azusa Publishing, L.L.C.

suspended by thongs fastened at the top of the pole to pegs inserted into slits in their chests for self affliction. Warriors strained to tear the skin and free the pegs, or had them cut out at dawn, when the dance ended. The scars on their chests were exhibited as trophies for the ordeal, but they would wear those scars for the rest of their lives. If the squaws joined in, they danced in the inner circle, but did not engage in the sun pole ritual.

Buffalo skulls were inserted by thongs between the ropes and the pegs. By the same rite a warrior chose self mutilation, by slashing his arms and legs, before going on the war trail.

Incantations and prayers were uttered. The Sioux Sun Dance was done similar to the Blackfeet Indian Sun Dance. The Sun Dance Ordeal was portrayed in the movie, "A Man Called Horse."

In the Scalp Dance, scalps hung from the scalp pole in the center of the circle. Sioux squaws (women) danced around the scalp pole in cadence to the eerie sound of the shaman's chanting and beating of the drum.

Sometimes, rattles or wooden mariachis accompanied the dancing. Participating in the Scalp Dance was the sacred duty of the Sioux squaws. The female dancers rose in the air and dropped down in a hopping step to the rhythm of the music.

A scalp was stretched around a willow branch fashioned into a hoop and attached to a willow pole decorated with beads, feathers, and colored with red ochre. A squaw, whose brother, husband or son was killed, relayed the story of his death, and a scalp said, "Whose enemy scalp is on my shoulder?" They all gave a shout and the dancing resumed. The scalp was then put back on the burial scaffold.

Warrior dancers did a mock scalp dance and wore braided grass symbolizing enemy scalps. Historians believe that the Assiniboine Indians (a lost Sioux tribe) were an offshoot of the Yanktonai. The Sioux word, *assnipwan* means "Stone Sioux," since they used red-hot boiling stones for cooking.

The story is that the two tribes were one, but divided in the 17th century in northern Canada; one group remained in place, while the other migrated to the plains to hunt bison. Euro-Americans came into contact with the Assiniboine in northern Canada in the 1600's, where they dwelled from Lake Nipigon to the Saskatchewan River.

The Yankton Sioux hunted buffalo in Montana Territory. The Siouan word for buffalo was *pte*. The southern group divided again into two bands some time before 1750. The Yankton remained in the Missouri Valley to hunt buffalo and the Yanktonai re-entered Canada across what the Indians called the "medicine" or "holy line" the arbitrary line dividing America and Canada.

The Plains Sioux were prolific sign talkers and were noted their use of sign language. The American Indian sign language is still used today, primarily at ceremonies, festivals and intertribal powwows.

Another form of communication the American Indians utilized was smoke signals which were used to send messages for miles from a lofty position on a hill or plateau. A huge bonfire was kindled. A damp blanket was placed over the smoldering fire and lifted to send messages by puffs of smoke that rose in the sky to signal the tribe of danger or of war. This way the Indians could communicate during warfare to know what the enemy was doing without their knowledge by a series of puffs of smoke. Indians used mirrors, after the white man, to send flashes to alert their band of danger or of attack.

#8 Squaw Carries Firewood
Courtesy of Azusa Publishing, L.L.C.

The Sioux Indians were hunters and gatherers and formed a powerful buffalo hunting society. Their culture encompassed the buffalo, horse and warfare. The Sioux bands of the Northern Plains were nomad buffalo hunters. They followed the movements of the buffalo herds and moved their villages behind the bison migration, continually during the spring, summer and fall.

Prior to the horse, the Sioux hunted buffalo on foot and closed in on the herd from downwind, as to not alert the herd of their presence and were careful not to scare the herd and cause a dangerous stampede. Some Plains Indians had lost their lives, after being gored by maddened buffaloes. Skilled hunters crawled among the wild buffalo, concealed beneath a wolf skin, a brave could stalk a buffalo and get a clean shot with his bow and arrow and not arouse suspicion. At times, a buffalo decoy was used to attract the dumb beasts.

The Sioux First Nation was formed of the confederacy. The confederacy was formed of tribes and bands made up the tribes. Extended family members made up bands. Bands sometimes were nonrelated, called composite groups, but often with blood-ties. The socio-political rule of the Sioux Indians was formed of a council of band chiefs. The tribe was governed by the council of band chiefs, who directed the tribal affairs, such as the hunt, war, and camp moves. There were seven band chiefs in the tribe originally, but in historic times the white man insisted they have just one chief to represent the tribe; so the band chose one chief for them to parley with.

Chieftains were chosen for character traits, as were sub-chiefs for their bravery in war, generosity and wisdom, as well as prowess on the hunt. The people had to be willing to be led. In the American Indian militia, a chief could choose a lieutenant to serve under him in battle.

Hunters chose a hunt chief or leader before the hunt. It was democratic rule by the people.

Bands of extended families made up of possibly 150 men, women and children followed the Sioux scouts in a procession behind the moving herd for days and weeks and camped near the buffalo herd. Bison were hunted and butchered, the meat jerked and hides worked by the squaws. The family came first; members of the community were cared for and food was shared.

The path for a young brave to become a man was to experience a vision in the wild (vision quest). He fasted, prayed, cleansed, mutilated himself and ultimately envisioned an animal or bird in the spirit realm. He burned sweet grass, and fanned the smoke over himself to gain purity.

The young Indian learned to count coup, (French for touch). He rode up to surprise the enemy in close contact and struck his foe with his quirt (small leather whip). This progressed into combat and warfare. Scalping was a ploy learned from the French. A warrior removed a circle of scalp and hair from his dead foe as a trophy.

There was division among the sexes. Men hunted; women gathered. The Sioux woman was the family matriarch and ruled over their domestic life. She owned the teepee and the contents inside the lodge. The woman cooked for the family, cared for the children and made the family's clothing from skins, using awls, bone eye needles, burins, perforators and gut for sewing.

Mothers carried their babies (papooses) in cradleboards on their backs while they worked. The cradleboard was a skin covered oval board decorated with porcupine quills or glass seed beads. The cradleboard could be transported by travois or hung from a saddle.

Women did the brunt of the work: tanned the hides, carried water and collected firewood. Squaws foraged for berries, nuts, roots, and seeds and gathered wild vegetables like wild celery, onions, potatoes, turnips and dug camas and other edible roots, while the men hunted game. They cached food in underground pits lined with rocks for storage and cooked the meals for the family. As nomads, they did not have the time to make basketry and pottery, but traded with other tribes and trading posts for these items.

Fire was produced from friction, by rubbing a fire stick between the palms or using a drill pump with a wooden shaft, drill cup and tinder. Plant fibers were used to make cordage in the manufacture of bags, netting and rope.

The Sioux were Indians of the plains and wore the full regalia of the Plains Indians. Squaws wore dresses and jackets of deerskin or trade cloth. The women donned deerskin dresses, with fringes, decorated with porcupine quills or dentalium shell beads and a belt. Necklaces of hair-pipe also were worn. Indian women often wore deer or elk skin skirts on summer days, with their breasts exposed. Squaws wore deerskin leggings from moccasins to the knees and wore their long hair loose with a head band or in braids.

Men wore their hair loose with a forelock that hung to the nose, or wore braids. Medicine Pipe men rolled their hair into a thick topknot, held with clay above the forehead like the Blackfeet Indians. Indians wore bear oil in their hair. They adorned their hair with beads, feathers and fur. Otter fur strips tied their braids. Hair brushes were made of porcupine quills supported by a wood handle and a wrap of rawhide; another brush was constructed of horse hair in a loop with a rawhide-wrapped handle. Hairstyle, garb and feathers helped identify one tribe from another.

Men's garb was made from soft deerskin, also. The men wore breech clouts (loin cloths), deerskin war-shirts (tunics) and moccasins. Leggings reached from the hips to the moccasins (bare at the buttocks), were fringed and decorated with beadwork, quillwork or painted.

Moccasins were made from the sheath of a deer's foreleg from one piece, hair on the inside, called the hock moccasin, formed naturally and sewn on one end. It was tied to lace; three pieces of leather were sewn together in the Freemont style. Hard soles were worn in summer and soft soles in winter.

The Sioux dyed porcupine quills various colors using plant pigments to adorn moccasins and leggings in colorful geometric designs. They decorated their moccasins with minute bright colored glass seed beads and porcupine quills after the arrival of the French and English traders.

Tatoos were common among the aborigines of the Plains. Both sexes wore tatoos on their bodies. Designs were tatooed on the arms, chests, and faces as a thing of beauty.

In winter bearskin, buffalo or rabbit fur robes were worn. The robes could be worn for warm outerwear in the winter cold. Buffalo sleeping robes made frigid winters tolerable. Buffalo robes were warm in winter.

Trade-blankets were also worn after the coming of the white man and the fur forts. A blanket Indian was an Indian who refused to accept the ways of the white man. Consequently, he wore the blanket in protest.

Firearms reached the Great Lakes region from Canada and the east coast through English and French fur traders, so the Chippewa (Ojibwa) Indians had firearms and horses early (bartered from traders which gave them superiority over the Sioux and drove them into Dakota Territory).

Militant Chippewa forced the Sioux to retreat, around 1760 into the Upper Missouri region because they had no guns. The Sioux moved westward onto the Great Plains, where they hunted, fished and farmed. The Great Plains in America reached from the Mississippi to the Rocky Mountains, and from Canada to the Gulf of Mexico, where millions of buffalo roamed.

The dinosaurs, the mammoth, mastodon elephants and other large species died off early and the theory that the largest animals were first to face extinction because of their size has long been accepted.

The early horse species had died off in America. Paleontologists theorize from the size of the skulls found that the first horses most likely were zebras. The "Hagerman Horse" in Idaho is such an example.

One theory is that wild horses were hunted by the Indians and eaten, as opposed to being ridden, and became extinct in America. The modern horse was transported to America by Spanish explorers from Europe. Ute Indians stole the Spaniard's mustangs and became the first Indians to possess horses, once thought to be big dogs.

One tribe was largely responsible for providing the Northwestern American Indians with horses. The southern Comanche stole horses from the Apache and Spanish colonists. After the Pueblo Revolt in 1680, horses ran wild in the desert. Comanches caught wild mustangs and amassed hundreds of ponies in a herd by raids. Some chiefs possessed herds over 1,000 horses.

Comanche Indians drove up to two thousand horses north at one time to distribute the mustangs to various tribes to populate the Northwest with the Spanish horses. One round trip took over two years to drive horses north and return to northern Texas.

Horses reached the Sioux in the mid 1800's, but records show some Sioux with the horse as early as 1700. Never having seen a horse, the Sioux called them medicine dogs, acquired horses from Northern Cheyenne and Mandan trade centers and bartered from trading posts. They hunted buffalo easily on horse-back as Plains Indians, militant warriors and buffalo hunters.

The Sioux amassed huge quantities of ponies from theft. Stealing a horse was known as counting coup. An Indian acquired great wealth in the number of horses he owned.

Once, a Sioux traded forty horses for one medicine pipe. On a moon-lit night riding with a Sioux raiding party, a brave could steal into an enemy camp, cut the thongs holding the horses and take them undetected. Crow Indians stole horses from the Sioux, but the shrewd Sioux stole them back.

The Sioux socio-political structure became a militant one. On horseback, the Sioux became a powerful foe. With horses and firearms, the Sioux became fierce warriors. The Sioux were compared to the Blackfeet and Comanche in fighting strength. They fought enemy tribes, white men and the U.S. Army to defend their hunting grounds.

In 1765, the mighty Sioux pushed the Kiowa Indians from the Black Hills and drove the Crow Indians from the Powder River country, and occupied it as their own.

In time, the Sioux dominated central Canada and the Northern Plains, from the Bighorn Mountains to the Minnesota River and from the Platte and Republican Rivers to the Upper Missouri. Powerful Blackfeet, Comanche and Sioux Indians ruled the Great Plains. It was difficult for other tribes to hunt buffalo in their territory.

The Sioux, like most American Indians, believed in spirit guides and that the mother earth, rocks, wind, sun, moon and stars all had a spirit (animism). The celestial orbs were their gods and they lived in harmony with nature. Dreams were important to the Sioux, who believed that the spirits spoke to them in dreams. Medicine men used dreams, trances and visions to contact the spirits.

The medicine man acted as an intermediary between the natural and supernatural worlds and used his magic to heal the sick, foretell the future and control spiritual forces. The medicine man led the medicine-bands, who assisted him in warding off evil and healing illness with chanting and prayer. Medicine men were feared because of their powers.

The Medicine Dance accompanied the sacred feast given by the medicine man. Men and women inducted into the order of the sacred mysteries dance were extended an invitation by messenger from the medicine man. As the guests arrived, the sacred medicine bag was opened, with ritual. The medicine man produced the pipe from the sacred medicine bag and puffed on the pipe, as he passed it around to the guests for all to smoke. When all had smoked, the shaman announced that the pipe was out.

One method of healing the sick used by shaman was to place his mouth on an area of pain or sickness and blow smoke from his pipe onto the body. He would then suck out the infirmity (evil spirit) from the body to heal the patient through his magic. Nature was the Shaman's pharmacy. Herbs, plants, roots, and tree bark made good medicine.

Many feathers were earned for valor. When a warrior took coup, he was honored by an eagle feather. After a seasoned warrior accrued enough eagle feathers, he fashioned a war bonnet. Hawk and eagle feathers made beautiful headdresses and costumes worn in dances, ceremonies and celebrations. Sometimes the Sioux caught young eagles and hawks and kept them in stick cages for their feathers.

Feathers were notched, painted or worn in a certain position to indicate the number of coups or if a warrior had taken a scalp. A brave usually wore one feather in his hair, sometimes, two. Feathers had meaning and were marked by notching or painting them to indicate feats in battle.

In the winter time, braves wore leather caps of badger, coyote or otter fur, with feathers or dyed porcupine quills. Caps were adorned with a buffalo horns on both sides made a fine war bonnet.

The Sioux caught grown eagles for their utility, since their feathers made fine war bonnets. The talons were crafted into strong charms for good medicine and the wing bones made fine whistles. A deep depression or a naturally formed pit covered with pine boughs was used as a pit trap. A rabbit was laid on the boughs as bait and the warrior carefully crawled in and waited.

When the catcher heard the eagle cry, as it lit on the rabbit, he quickly reached up and grabbed hold of the great bird's legs and pulled with all of his might to bring it down. The bird's talons raked his wrists and chest, but he held on. The huge bird flapped its wings and nearly knocked him down; the catcher grabbed its head, placed both knees on its body and twisted its neck as hard as he could. At last, the eagle fell limp. The Sioux was exhausted from the struggle, but had captured a majestic eagle.

The young men learned to shoot a bow early. The Sioux Indians fashioned fine bows and arrows of ash, cedar, juniper, osage and yew wood measuring about four feet in length. Men hunted game with bow and arrows. 2,000 years ago, the bow and arrow replaced the atlatl. Early man utilized the atlatl for thousands of years previous.

Animal skin was sometimes wrapped around the bows for strength and rattlesnake skin was a popular adornment used. Bowstrings were normally made from animal gut, called sinew.

Arrows were fashioned from willow or any of the above woods and tipped with arrow heads made of bone, stone, or wood. The shaft was heated and straightened, then smoothed and polished for an arrow, using grooved stone abraders, smoothers and lastly, polishers. Indians flaked stone arrowheads from flint and then inserted them into a slit at the end of the shaft, glued and wrapped it with sinew. Eagle feathers were fletched to the arrow. Prehistoric knives were flaked from chert with bone or wood handles. Scalp knives were wooden handled butcher knives traded from forts.

Quivers made of cougar or other animal skin held their arrows. War shields were made of tough buffalo hide taken from the neck region to deflect arrows. The very toughest part of the skin was used for a war shield. The circular piece was dried over a pit fire, while it was wet. Holes burned around the edge were used to lash the hide to the frame, made from a sapling tied into a circle for a shield with eagle feathers attached.

War shields held sacred power from the gods; personal symbols were painted on war shields, teepees and sometimes clothing. The warrior was outfitted with bow, arrows, knife, lance, tomahawk, war shield and rifle.

American Natives were stone-age people. Stone lithic tools had handles of antler, bone, horn or wood and were fastened with sinew. Stone tools were popular. Adzes, arrowheads, awls, drill points, gravers, hide scrapers, knives and shaft scrapers were chipped (flaked) from basalt, chert and obsidian. Hand axes and shovels were fashioned of larger cores.

Hammers, tomahawks and war-clubs were monolithic with a deep groove or flaked heads, hafted on with strips of rawhide onto wooden handles. Ball clubs were (baseball sized) round stones sewn into leather with a strap, swung around the head.

Tomahawk pipes were trade-blades adorned with beaded pendants utilized as a pipe to be smoked or a weapon for war, or were pipes fashioned of clay and made a prize trade item.

Wild buffalo originally roamed freely in a large triangle between northwestern, Canada, in the north, south into Mexico, and eastward to the Appalachians. Millions of bison roamed the plains before the turn of the 19th Century, but nearly disappeared due to over-kill.

The buffalo was America's largest mammal, reaching ten feet in length, weighing a ton and able to run 40 miles an hour. Its fur was long in winter and short during the summer. The only predator of the buffalo was the black bear, brown bear, cougar, and packs of coyotes and wolves. A single wolf could mingle with the herd unthreatened, but a wolf pack could bring down a single buffalo.

Male and female bison herds migrated in season to find annual grasses. These grazing ruminants fed on grasses, sedges, and occasionally berries and lichen. Because buffalo ate grasses down so short in little time, they had to migrate. They used their head and horns to clear vegetation of snow.

The two herds did not mix until mating season. Buffalo are polygamous in the mating season. Bulls fought each other for mating rites. Dominant bulls maintain their harem in season.

When the Sioux moved onto the Great Plains, they adopted the plains culture of Indian, horse and buffalo. The Sioux diet consisted mainly of buffalo. Buffalo meat was a delicacy, at the top of the food chain. The buffalo was their world and provided most of the Sioux Indian's needs. The buffalo provided food, skins for their tents, clothing and moccasins, buffalo horns and hooves for religious ceremonies, even buffalo chips for their campfires.

One hunting method of the Sioux was the buffalo surround. They formed a large circle around a herd of wild buffalo, moved in closing the circle and shot the beasts with bow and arrows before butchering them.

The buffalo corral was crafted in a V shape on a down slope. A medicine man crawled among the herd, under a buffalo robe bleating like a baby calf; the dumb animals had poor eyesight and followed him into the trap.

The buffalo jump method to hunt bison was a communal undertaking used by the Sioux. Stone lanes were built on a cliff adjoining a bluff. Rock barriers were built along the sides forming a kind of runway. The Shaman gave a war whoop, waved a blanket and startled the herd, grazing nearby, to stampede over the cliff. Processing stations below were used to butcher the bison for the meat and to remove the hides. The bison killed were shared by the whole tribe.

Another hunting expedition buffalo were killed using the bow and arrow, a lance or rifle. The hunt leader fired a rifle shot into the air stampeding a herd of buffalo. The warrior-hunter, mounted on his best buffalo horse, streaked to catch up to a fleeing buffalo running 40 miles an hour. The Sioux hunter spurred his horse until he was right beside the grunting buffalo and drew back his bow. The arrow was aimed between the ribs or directly behind the shoulder. The shaft penetrated the beast's lung. It labored to breathe, as it lumbered along and finally snorted and stumbled into a heap. Pack horses or mules were used to transport the meat and hides back to the encampment. Sometimes the meat was jerked in the field for consumption later.

The hunters butchered the buffalo and the women stretched the hides and staked them down and worked arduously to scrape the hides and remove all of the flesh and fat with stone hide scrapers. Squaws fleshed the hides with stone hide scrapers, which were then tanned using bison brains or other methods producing warm sleeping robes. Cow buffalo were taken in Indian summer and slaughtered before winter arrived, in order to make robes before the cold season.

Excess meat was jerked and ground fine in a mortar and pestle or a buffalo skin mortar with a mano to nearly a powder and mixed with animal fat and chokecherries. It was then made into cakes, called pemmican and was preserved in woven sagebrush fiber bags used to store foods underground.

The Sioux ate the rich red buffalo meat mainly, but ate some fowl, fish and other meats. Squaws did the cooking and preparation. Fresh meat was cooked in a stew or roasted on a spit or cooked in a paunch of an animal, clay or rawhide vessels or by using red-hot stones from a camp fire in a pitch-sealed water-basket, as water simmered meat was added to cook. Meat was broiled on spits. Three flat rocks (fire-dogs) supported a cook pot on a pit fire.

Before tipis, subterranean pit houses were built for lodgings. Walls were sapling uprights, covered with earth and a roof of thatched rye grass. A hearth provided heat for cooking and warmth.

The Plains tipi (teepee) is a Lakota Sioux Indian word meaning "a place where one lives" sometimes called a wigwam (an Abenaki Indian word for hut). A tipi is a tent constructed over numerous lodge poles in a conical shaped framework and tied near the top, covered with buffalo skins and held down with rocks. Hides served as the flooring. Buffalo fur blankets kept them warm in the winter in addition heated rocks were placed under foot to add warmth. Canvas was later used for tipi coverings.

By Sioux tradition the mother owned the tipi and its contents. The residence was near the wife's family (matrilocal) and the lineage, and passed down through the mother's line (matrilineal).

Using two tipi poles, a travois could be constructed to haul their tent and goods behind a horse. A horse was also used to pull a sledge laden with goods like hides to cover a teepee, goods and infants. Using additional poles, a tipi (photo, pg 21) could be erected in little time. Teepees were collapsible, portable and very efficient.

Sioux bands had used domestic dogs for work dogs with a travois (a sledge) to transport moderate loads of goods: hides, jerky and meat for hundreds of years. Horses also pulled the travois to transport goods, circa 1700 A.D., but the Indians continued to use dogs.

The wickiup (photo, pg 5) was a cone-shaped hut, covered with brush or matting. 'The Sioux also erected temporary shelters when they hunted and gathered food, with upright poles tied at the top. The thatch hut was similar in construction to the tipi, constructed of long willow poles, tied at the top in a conical configuration. (photo, pg 36) The framework was covered with sewn matting thatch.

When an Indian girl began puberty, she spent the time of her menses in a hut, called a menstrual hut, isolated on the village perimeter. She bathed and practiced spiritual cleansing by sprinkling sage or sweet grass on the coals of a fire and drew the smoke toward her with the motion of her hands, breathing it in. A small ceremony was usually held for her rite-of-passage.

Birthing huts were similar for child birth. Separate huts were used as well for child bearing, in a hut outside the village for about 30 days. Sioux Indian babies weren't always born in these huts. Sometimes the mother went into a remote area of a forest for privacy to have her child alone.

The communal sweat lodge was mostly used by the men in the village and was a social thing to bathe and boast of their feats in battle and hunting. The Sioux built sweat lodges and poured water on hot stones to make steam. They burned sage, wafted the sweet smoke toward themselves for self cleansing , and entered the steam bath and remained there a long time as the sweat ran from their bodies. They emerged from the steam bath, jogged to the nearest lake or stream and plunged into the ice cold water to keep fit.

Three great chiefs emerged from the ranks of the Teton Sioux tribe, an Oglala Sioux named, Red Cloud (photo, pg 84 etc.) and another Oglala, called Crazy Horse. The third chief was a Hunkpapa Sioux named, Sitting Bull (photos, pg 110, etc.)

Red Cloud was born on the Platte River, circa 1822, near present-day North Platte, Nebraska, was orphaned at an early age and raised by his uncle, Smoke. Red Cloud (Makhpiya-Luta) was just 15 when he rode in a war party

#9. Wichita Grass Hut
Courtesy of Western History Collections,
University of Oklahoma Libraries

and counted coup on the Pawnee and, at 16, took his first scalp. Red Cloud raided a Crow village and took 50 horses. At age 20, he killed a rival Oglala chief over a dispute and was skilled fighting the Crow, Pawnee, and Shoshoni and became a great Oglala war-chief.

Crazy Horse and Sitting Bull were born the same year. Crazy Horse was born on Rapid Creek in 1831. The parents of Crazy Horse were members of the Oglala band of the Dakota Sioux tribe. They were Plains Indians, dependent on the buffalo. He was given the name, of Tashunka-Uitko at birth.

Sioux tradition tells us *the day that Crazy Horse was born, a wild horse raced through his village, a sign and an omen of the greatness of Crazy Horse and his impending name.* As a youth he was called "Curly." When he came of age, he went into the wild for his vision quest and had a vision.

He saw a horse, whose hooves did not touch the ground. It floated, galloped and changed colors as did the attire of Crazy Horse. He rode freely, seeing grass, sky and trees and knew from his vision, his name was "Crazy Horse." While fighting the Grass Lodge People, Curly courageously earned his name, "Crazy Horse," (the same as his father).

Crazy Horse had a dream when he was about 20 years old. He dreamed he saw himself with trailing, unbraided hair, adorned with the feather of a red hawk, and a smooth stone behind his ear. From then on Crazy horse fought with a river pebble behind his left ear in a leather thong. He sprinkled dust over himself and his horse for power (from legend).

Crazy Horse was made one of four "shirt wearers," of the Oglala band, a great honor. He was a mystic and interpreted dreams, and misunderstood. Crazy Horse was a type of medicine man, his life surrounded by prophetic dreams. He was a holy man as much as a shaman and a loner among the Sioux; he never let a photographer take his picture; he believed that the camera would capture his own soul. No artist ever painted Crazy Horse.

Crazy Horse loved his childhood sweetheart, the beautiful Black Buffalo Woman, but the union was spoiled by an arranged marriage agreement between her parents and the parents of No Water, a member of Red Cloud's band. Crazy Horse came back from the war trail to learn she had married No Water, who refused to divorce her. Crazy Horse claimed his bride regardless and No Water threatened to cut off her nose, to spite him.

Black Buffalo Woman and Crazy Horse were together once more. They held deep love for each other. For a short time Crazy Horse was with his beloved. Then, No Water burst into their teepee and waved a pistol in the air. It fired and the slug tore under the skin and lodged in the cheek of Crazy Horse. He was disgraced and his shirt wearer rank was stripped from him. Black Buffalo Woman had no recourse but to return to No Water.

He rebounded by devoting his time to his role as war chief. The wild warrior Crazy Horse was very brave and daring. He was a tactical genius on the battlefield and a natural born leader and chief. Crazy Horse believed one did not sell the land where all living things walked. The Sioux admired Crazy Horse; others loathed him out of jealousy.

Sitting Bull was born, circa 1831, in a teepee on the Grand River to Sitting Bull and Her-Holy-Door, who carried her baby in a cradle board on her back and could work at the same time, her hands free. Sitting Bull had a six year old sister, Good Feather, and another sister born later named Brown Shawl Woman. Gall was his adopted brother; Fool Dog was his half brother.

Sitting Bull's birth name was Jumping Badger. He was very deliberate in his movements. His companions nicknamed him, "Slow," although he was unbeaten in every foot race. His father gave him the name, *Tantanka Iyotanka*, Sitting Bull in the Sioux tongue.

Sitting Bull's father was quite wealthy and owned a large herd of horses. He was a medicine man and chief. He had two younger brothers, Looks-for-Him-in-a-Tent, and Four Horns who were chiefs.

In 1834, the American Fur Company constructed the original Fort Laramie on the Oregon Trail, inhabited by fur trappers, traders, squaw men (mostly French fur traders married to Indian women) and Indians. Forts in the Laramie River region competed for the fur trade. Fort Platte was a rival fort.

In 1835, Marcus Whitman and Samuel Parker, missionaries to the Indians, arrived at Fort Laramie in the company of a number of fur traders. In 1836, Narcissa Whitman and Eliza Spalding, missionary wives, were the first white women to cross America in a covered wagon and visit Fort Laramie. A friendly band of Sioux happened to arrive at the fort for trade and honored the two missionaries by performing the Buffalo Dance for them.

In 1838, a smallpox epidemic reduced the Assiniboine numbers by two thirds. In 1842, wagon trains dotted the horizon. Miners, railroad workers, buffalo hunters, settlers and the U.S. Cavalry followed

Sitting Bull all but grew up on a horse. As a brave, he did trick riding. He could pick up an object off the ground from horseback or pull a friend up behind him from the ground and fire arrows under the horse's neck, or lay prone, shielded from enemy arrows, holding only on to its mane and by locking his legs around the horse's hind quarters and was safer in combat.

At age ten, Sitting Bull killed his first buffalo and began his vision quest, when he was twelve at the age of maturity. The four day ordeal was the test of manhood. At the age of 14, Sitting Bull knocked a Crow brave off his horse with his tomahawk, counted coup and earned a white eagle feather.

In 1846, at age fifteen, his band was camped along the Musselshell River. They discovered Flathead Indians spying on them. Sitting Bull rode in a party of fifteen braves to investigate, but was ambushed; he rode hard and met the attackers head on amongst flying arrows, routing the enemy, but received a foot wound which he carried through life, but earned a red eagle feather for his bravery.

In 1849, gold was discovered in California; thousands of miners clamored westward to the gold digs, moving across Sioux land. September 9, 1850, California joined the Union and 20,000,000 buffalo grazed the Plains, white men crossed the plains and deprived them of their food sources. The starving Indians attacked the miner's settlements for food and supplies.

Fort Laramie saw many thousands of Conestoga wagons pass through, and became a popular place for the Indians who put up their teepees. The Oregon Trail and the Mormon Trail both ran through Sioux country.

The U.S. government purchased Fort Laramie on the North Platte River in Wyoming for a military post in 1849. Indians called it "Soldier Town."

Kicking Bear (Mato Wanataka) (photo, pg 66) was born an Oglala Sioux Indian in 1850. His father was Black Fox, his mother, Woodpecker. He married the daughter of Chief Big Foot and paid the bride price with stolen Crow horses.

40

Bride-price was mostly paid in horses, tied in front of the teepee of the bride to be. A man could steal a wife, if approved by the society, but Sitting Bull did not steal his bride. His people mostly practiced monogamy. Sitting Bull matured as a warrior and acquired a wife in 1851. His marriage at first was monogamous, but Sitting Bull took more wives later.

On August 5, 1851, Chief Little Crow of the Santee Sioux signed a treaty with the federal government that ceded most of the Sioux territory in Minnesota to the United States. The Fort Laramie Treaty of 1851 determined the territory of the Sioux Nation to be from Canada to the Republican River (in Kansas) on the south and the Bighorn Mountains on the west to the eastern Wisconsin River. Assiniboines signed the treaty in 1851, limiting hunting. They hunted bison in Montana and camped by Fort Benton.

Father Jean Pierre De Smet was the first Roman Catholic missionary to the Sioux and other tribes along the Platte River and the Upper Missouri River region. The Indians called him Black Robe, because of his attire. Father De Smet had a soft spot in his heart for the Sioux people. He liked their courage, but disliked the cruelty.

Sitting Bull joined the elite (Midnight) Strong Heart and Kit-fox societies when he was 21, circa 1852, with Crow King and Gall. His best friends were Black Bird, Brave Thunder, Gall, and Strikes-the-Thunder. The Kit Fox society held festivities dressed in colorful costumes and painted their bodies. Most Plains tribes had similar societies.

Sitting Bull communed with nature and had dreams and visions. He possessed supernatural powers to interpret them. Sitting Bull became a medicine man loved by the Sioux, a deeply religious holy man, who foretold success of the hunt or in war. Sitting Bull was a wise medicine man who could predict a hot summer or a mild winter for the dance.

In 1853, through California legislation, the government illegally confiscated all the Indians' land and moved them onto reservations under military guard. Using near genocidal methods, the populations of the Native Americans were reduced from 150,000 in 1849 down to only 30,000 in 1870.

Crazy Horse dreamed of an incident between the Sioux and the white man that troubled him and in 1854, a Minneconjou named "High Forehead," shot a Mormon's cow near Fort Laramie and led to mistrust and bloodshed.

After the incident near Fort Laramie, Army, Lt. John Grattan decided to teach the Sioux a lesson. He led 34 soldiers with two cannons to annihilate them and rode to the Sioux camp. Lt. Grattan boldly led his company into the Sioux village near the mouth of the Snake River and by using a drunken interpreter, demanded that they surrender the one who killed the stray cow.

Chief Conquering Bear refused, as all hell broke loose; the Brule began firing. Grattan's men opened fire killing the chief.

Young Crazy Horse was a witness. The lieutenant had made a big mistake, because quickly the Brule warriors surrounded and overpowered the soldiers, killing his entire company. Lt. Grattan's unit never returned to Fort Laramie. All 35 of the soldiers' bodies were later found scalped, left by the Sioux; the hot-headed lieutenant had cost them their lives. Crazy Horse's dream had become reality.

#10. One Bull, Nephew of Sitting Bull
Courtesy of Azusa Publishing, L.L.C.

The Battle of Blue Water (Ash Hollow), Nebraska was a major clash between U.S. Soldiers and Sioux Indians to teach them a lesson for the Grattan Massacre.

Colonel Harney headed a column of 600 men that left Fort Leavenworth, Kansas to engage the Sioux and avenge the deaths of Lieutenant Grattan and company. Troops reached the Brule village of Little Thunder in Blue Water Valley September 3, 1855. The Sioux saw them coming and scattered. At battle's end, four soldiers were killed and seven were wounded.

The Brule Sioux and Northern Cheyenne retreated through Sioux country to Fort Pierce on the Missouri River, where they spent the winter of 1855-1856. Sioux aggression was almost non-existent for a decade. The Great Council of the Lakota Nation was held during the summer of 1857.

Sitting Bull became a war chief and led the Sioux against the Blackfeet, Crow, Pawnee, and Shoshoni tribes. He led the Hunkpapa band to fight the Blue Coats. In 1857, the Midnight Strong Hearts Society made Sitting Bull war chief of the Hunkpapas, head chief of the Teton Sioux Nation.

Sitting Bull's wife, Light Hair, died in childbirth in 1857; their son lived, but died of disease four years later. Sitting Bull adopted One Bull, the second son of his sister, Good Feather, wife of Minneconjou Chief Makes Room, and raised him as his own. White Bull, the oldest, remained with them.

After Light Hair died, Sitting Bull took two wives: Red Woman, who bore him a son and Snow-on-Her, who gave birth to two daughters. Sitting Bull's mother, sister and her son dwelled with him.

In 1857, Sitting Bull took an Assiniboine boy to raise after a skirmish with the Assiniboine; some Assiniboine and eight Sioux died.

Swift Cloud captured a young brave and was about to kill him. It touched Sitting Bull's heart when, the boy cried, "older brother," and embraced him.

In 1858, Sitting Bull stole a horse with a lump on its jaw from a white man and called it "Bloated Jaw," his best horse to hunt and in war. Legend tells us that Sitting Bull killed four or five bison before they scattered.

Sitting Bull was an expert horseman and rode bareback, with only a bridle. He wore a loin cloth and moccasins, with two feathers in his hair and red war paint. He had an ornate painted war shield of tough, buffalo hide with sacred powers and four eagle feathers hanging down. His favorite weapon was his lance and shield, but carried bow, arrows, rifle, knife and tomahawk.

In 1859, the Hunkpapa had camped at Rainey Buttes along the Cannonball and were moving north, as 50 Crow warriors attacked. Swift Hawk counted coup on a brave. A Crow warrior crossed a creek, pursued by Sitting Crow, Grindstone, and Knife King; they counted coup on him.

When one Crow brave's horse gave out, he was surrounded by Sioux warriors. Jumping Badger was stabbed and killed. Sitting Bull avenged his father's death, but the Sioux warriors had to pull the outraged Sitting Bull off him.

June 20, 1861, Crazy Horse went on the war path with his Oglala band against the Shoshoni, old enemies of the Sioux people. The attack took the life of the son of Washakie, Chief of the Green and Wind River Shoshoni, who claimed six enemy scalps taken. Washakie was a peace chief, who won a peace medal and a silver saddle from the president. His daughter married Jim Bridger. Bridger was the frontiersman, who discovered the Great Salt Lake and opened many trails.

#11. Washakie's Village
Courtesy of the Smithsonian Institute

SIOUX INDIAN MYTHOLOGY
WHITE BUFFALO CALF WOMAN BRINGS THE PIPE

The Sioux believed their god *Wakan Tanka* created the buffalo for their people and believed it to be sacred, completing their life style. The white buffalo was a rarity, eulogized by the people of the Plains. Many stories were told of the white buffalo. This story came from Sioux Indian legend and told of the white buffalo woman, who brought the sacred pipe in the medicine bag to the Sioux 2,000 years ago.

~~~~~~~~~

One day, two Sioux warriors hunted buffalo in the sacred Black Hills in South Dakota. Then, an animal moved towards them; it was a white buffalo calf, a color sacred to the Sioux. As it came toward them, it turned into a beautiful young Indian girl. One warrior had bad thoughts just then and the girl told him to step forward. When he did, a dark cloud enveloped him and removed the flesh and blood from his bones.

The other warrior knelt to pray. As he prayed, the Indian girl told him to go back to his people and warn them that in four days she would bring them the sacred bundle. He returned and called together the elders, leaders and all the people in a circle and told them told them what the beautiful young Indian girl had told him that she would appear on the fourth day.

As it was told, a cloud came on the fourth day and the white buffalo calf stepped out of it. As the cloud touched the earth, it became a beautiful, young woman who carried the sacred bundle.

As the woman entered the circle of nations, she sang a sacred song and brought the bundle to the people, spending four days among them and taught them the meaning of the sacred bundle. She also taught them of the seven sacred ceremonies, beginning with the sweat lodge (purification), child naming, adoption, healing, marriage, vision quest and Sun dance ceremonies.

She taught the people songs and traditional ways and instructed the people that as long as they performed ceremonies, they would remain caretakers of the sacred land; and as long as the people respected it, they would never die and always live. Legend was that the white buffalo could transform itself into a white hawk, white fox, or a beautiful woman and, if killed, was sacrificed to the Sioux Indian gods.

When she left, the White Buffalo Woman promised to return one day for the bundle and left the sacred bundle in their keeping.

The folk tale of the Great Spirit Wakan Tanka (the Great Mystery) told how "Grandfather" created the world and a great flood, and how he broke a piece of the wall to made a sacred red pipe, for the color of his people.

The stone pipe legend told how the Great Spirit puffed on the sacred pipe and blew puffs of smoke to Mother Earth, the four directions, the sun, moon, and stars and exhaled a huge puff of smoke, glazing the rock for miles.

As the great flood water rose around the young maiden, she caught the foot of a giant bird flying over. It carried her off to a nearby cliff. She gave birth to twins. Their father was the war eagle. They peopled the earth.

~~~~~~~~~~

#12. Sacred White Buffalo
Courtesy of Azusa Publishing, L.L.C.

#13. Sacajawea, "Bird Woman"
Idaho State Historical Museum, Boise, Idaho
Author Photo

Chapter Two
PALEFACES

By 1800 western America remained a wilderness and few Americans had been west of the Mississippi. In the early 1800's, Europeans began arriving in North America east of the Mississippi. The white settlers had a different idea about land ownership and pressured the government to acquire Indian lands for their use to build homes and plant crops.

1801, Thomas Jefferson became President; he sent a covert message to Congress asking that trade be established with the Indians and urged them to raise livestock, grow crops and enter into industry. The Constitution states that Congress has authority to regulate commerce with Indian tribes.

In 1803, the President signed the Louisiana Purchase with France, doubling the size of America, west from the Mississippi to the Rockies, and between Canada and Mexico was added and he wanted a team to explore the land west of the Rocky Mountains to the Pacific Ocean.

Jefferson asked Congress for monies for the mission, but Congress could only raise $2500 to finance the expedition. Jefferson authorized the military expedition of Captain Meriwether Lewis and Captain William Clark in 1803, to lead an odyssey of the Corp of Discovery with 31 army corps and hired men to trek cross-country to the Pacific Ocean.

Explorers preceded the fur traders in the early 1800's. The Corp journeyed from St. Louis and embarked up the Missouri River, where Clark met his old interpreter, Pierre Dorian Sr. and was introduced to his son, Pierre, Jr. who had been trading furs with the Yankton Sioux Indians.

Pierre Sr. married a Sioux Indian; their son was a French-Sioux cross, who was an interpreter for Wilson Price Hunt, crossing America. His wife, Marie was an Omaha Sioux, who gained fame traveling with the Hunt party.

Clark's party paddled up the Upper Missouri in what is now North Dakota and reached a Sioux speaking Mandan village. They met Toussaint Charbonneau, a French-Indian trapper Clark hired to interpret and his Shoshoni wife, Sacajawea (Bird Woman) (photo pg. 50). They reached the Pacific in 1804 and returned the next year and met Sioux Indians while passing through.

In 1804, the U.S. government began Indian removal east of the Mississippi River to Indian Territory in parts of Nebraska, Colorado, Kansas, Wyoming and most of Oklahoma. Land was set aside for Indian removal from their ancestral lands to make way for non-Indians to settle there.

French fur traders arrived, followed by the English and their soldier forts. Traders bartered axes, steel arrow heads, blankets, cloth, coffee, glass beads, guns and ammunition, horses, kettles, knives, mirrors, pipes, powder horns, and tobacco in exchange for furs in trade from the Indians. Metal tools replaced stone tools, as the old ways began to disappear. The Sioux engaged in hunting and trapping for the furs and hides and brought antelope, bear, beaver, buffalo and deer skins for trade. Trade was important to the Sioux.

The English and French established forts west of the Continental Divide; the Northwest Company built three fur trade forts in Idaho by 1812. Donald McKenzie constructed Fort Nez Perce on the Columbia in 1818.

These forts supplied the Indians with all kind of goods to survive. In exchange the Indians brought all manner of animal furs for trade.

Congress appointed agents to deal with the Indian tribes, in 1818. The Hudson Bay Company bought the Northwest Company in 1822. March 11, 1824, the U.S. Secretary of War established the Bureau of Indian Affairs.

In 1825, John McLaughlin was delegated to construct Fort Vancouver in Oregon Territory. Many fur and military forts followed. The Indians called them soldier forts.

On December 3, 1828, Andrew Jackson was elected President of the United States of America. The Indian Office was established in 1824 by the Secretary of War and later became the Bureau of Indian Affairs.

May 28, 1830, U.S. Congress passed the Indian Removal Act authorizing the president to negotiate with eastern American Indian tribes for their removal west of the Mississippi.

Over time, the eastern American Indians were conquered by the Army and forced to relinquish millions of acres to the U. S. government east of the Mississippi and were pushed off their land. The Eastern Sioux and the Winnebago Indians were tribes included in the removal. At the turn of the 19th century the "Western Frontier" was a wilderness, inhabited only by American Indians and wild animals.

In the 1800's, 13 million buffalo grazed across present day Montana. One herd migrated from southern Canada and wintered in Montana. Another large herd came in from Colorado, Nebraska and Wyoming Territories.

In 1829, the American Fur Company established the Fort Union trading post, located at the mouth of the Yellowstone.

On March 18, 1831, Chief Justice John Marshall characterized Indian groups within the United States as domestic dependent nations.

May 10, 1832, the Black Hawk War was fought in Illinois and Wisconsin. This war ended hostile Indian resistance east of the Mississippi.

In 1840, the Southern Arapaho and Southern Cheyenne Indians made peace with the Comanche, Kiowa and Plains Apache Indians.

In 1840, Father De Smet visited Fort La Ramee and saw forty Cheyenne lodges near the fort for the fur trade. Father De Smet found the Cheyenne Indians peaceable.

Wagon trains began moving along the Oregon Trail circa 1842, along the long 2,000 mile journey west from St. Louis across the Oregon Trail and stopped at Fort Laramie. Wagons lined the Oregon Trail as far as the eye could see. River boats churned up the rivers. Chinese workers built the rails across the prairie for the "Iron Horse" and the Union Pacific Railroad.

The government sent word for miles around to the Arikara, Arapaho, Assiniboine, Cheyenne, Crow, Hidatsa and Sioux Indian chiefs to come to Fort Laramie for peace talks; there was to be feasting, presents and they would smoke the pipe of peace, but the Comanche and Kiowa rejected the idea, since they had too many horses and mules to risk the Crow and Sioux stealing them. The Pawnee also refused, because their Sioux enemies would be there.

At the Treaty of Fort Laramie in 1851, Cheyenne and Sioux Chiefs, Spotted Tail, Roman-Nose, Old-Man-Afraid-of-His Horses, Lone Horn, Pipe, Whistling Elk and Slow Bull (page 62.) all met with commissioners to sign the most important peace treaty with the Indians of the 19th century, signed by the Arapaho, Cheyenne, Crow, Sioux and other Plains tribes. The Laramie Treaty was a major step in the peace process with the Plains Indians tribes. The treaty was soon broken by the white man and the Indians rebelled.

Father De Smet attended the 1851 the Treaty Council involving 10,000 Indians. He greeted Indians he knew and baptized many more. The treaty took their lands, made peace, and allowed passage across their lands.

Pony Express Riders rode from St. Joseph, Missouri, deliveries beginning April 3, 1860, while stage coaches crossed their lands carrying mail. The Army built forts and skirmished with the Indians.

Colorado Territory during the 1860's was gold mining territory, home to tens of thousands of men mining gold. Thousands of miners flocked to the mining camps. The Arapaho and Cheyenne Indians were being overrun by miners encroaching on Indian lands, which outraged them. Sod busters, stage-lines, wagon trains, and U.S. Army troops seemed to be everywhere; as the white man flooded their lands, Indians went on the warpath. Indian Wars broke out; angry war parties of Arapaho and Cheyenne warriors attacked, joined in their raids by the Comanche, Kiowa, and Sioux. A family was massacred by Indians in the Colorado War of 1864.

The Colorado Territory Governor, John Evans wanted the Indians hunting grounds for white settlement, but the Indians refused to sell. Gov. Evans asked Lt. Colonel John Chivington to stop the Indian action. Chivington was known as an Indian hater, who wanted to see them all dead and enjoyed attacking the Indian villages, razing them to the ground for sport, in early Colorado and Kansas Territory.

Black Kettle was chief of a band of 600 Southern Cheyenne and Plains Arapaho Indians and was a peace chief and advocated peace with no more bloodshed. He informed Fort Lyons of the location of his village, before he left to hunt buffalo, leaving the women and children.

In the autumn of 1864, Kit Carson led the New Mexico Volunteers against the Kiowa and Comanche Indians at Adobe Walls. In four days Colonel Carson had won a great victory. One hundred fifty warriors were dead, 175 lodges burned. Carson's lost three men dead and 25 wounded.

Five days after the Battle of Adobe Walls, Colonial Chivington (a Methodist preacher) reported to Fort Lyons and was informed that Cheyenne Chief Black Kettle had already surrendered. He disregarded the news and rode ahead of his column toward Black Kettle's village. On November 29, 1864, 750 volunteers of the 3rd Colorado Cavalry, under his command attacked the sleeping village of Cheyenne Indians at Sand Creek, an American flag and a white flag flew over their camp. The murderous Chivington knew this, but charged anyway. One hundred sixty three Cheyenne and Arapaho were attacked, mostly females and children. His troops assaulted, raped, and murdered these innocent Indians, 110 of the victims woman and children.

The fight was known as the Battle of Sand Creek, but General Nelson A. Miles wrote a letter to the Commissioner of Indian Affairs, attesting to the fact that the battle should be renamed, the Sand Creek Massacre. Later, after two congressional hearings, Governor Evans was removed from office and John Chivington was exiled for his sins. October 14, 1865, Southern Cheyenne Indians chiefs signed a treaty that ceded Colorado Territory to the U.S. as a result of the incident at Sand Creek.

Miles was an expert Indian fighter, yet a friend to the Indians. He understood them and respected the Indian. General Miles had lived with the Sioux and never saw more brotherhood, charity and kindness, anywhere. The Indians nicknamed Miles "Bear Coat," for his heavy bear fur winter coat.

Chapter Three
SIOUX ALLIES

The Cheyenne are believed to have been Woodland Indians who migrated west from the Great Lakes region in the late 17th century into Minnesota. Their ancestors possibly crossed the Bering Straits, Alaska and Canada into the Great Lakes. They were called *Tsistsistas* or "the people."

Legend told how the Cheyennes migrated west along the Missouri onto the plains in the Dakotas and Minnesota on the Red River in the 18th century and became associated with the Arikara, Hidatsa, and Mandan people. On first contact, they were said to be fish eaters and grew some corn in the Upper Missouri country, while hunting the buffalo. They combined farming and hunting, grew beans, corn and squash and lived in semi-subterranean earth lodges. They had matrilineal clans; newlyweds lived with the bride's parents.

The Cheyenne were Algonquian speakers, the largest speaking stock in America and a vast speaking family over a large area. Over time, the Cheyenne split into two groups: the Northern Cheyenne lived on the Northern Plains and the Southern Cheyenne dwelled on the Southern Plains.

Ceremonies of the Animal Dance (*Massaum*), the Sacred Arrows Dance and the Sun Dance were all festivals of the Cheyenne Indians. The three ceremonies were held in off years. The Animal Dance hunting ritual had been brought down the Sacred Mountain to insure plenty of meat for the tribe. A priest instructed a man and his wife (sponsors) in the arrangements and rituals of the dance, which lasted four days and nights. A double lodge was erected.

14.
Cheyenne Sun Dancers
Courtesy of Azusa Publishing Company, LLC

Dancers picked their favorite animals to mimic. Men from different groups masqueraded and danced, imitating an animal: antelope, bear, buffalo, cougar, coyote or deer. The Bowstring Society or Contrary Warriors created a mock hunt. "Contrary warriors" danced backwards and clowned. The Cheyenne warriors proved their prowess and power over the animal in the hunt.

The Renewal of the Sacred Arrow Ritual was a social activity of the men that lasted eight days. The Ceremonial Circle of teepees surrounded the ten Cheyenne bands' lodges within, the shape representing the summer moon. Teepee openings faced the east to allow in the warm morning rays of the sun.

In the center of the Great Circle stood the Sacred Arrow Lodge and behind it was the Offering Lodge, teepee of the sponsors of the ceremony. A member, who planned the ceremony and kept the Sacred Medicine met with all of the Cheyenne camps, where they smoked the sacred pipe.

The Lodge of the Sacred Arrow Keeper stood to the right of the Sacred Arrow Lodge. Music from drums and singing came from painted warriors. Sacred arrows were presented by Maiyun, the mythical hero.

Sweet Medicine, a brave warrior and his wife went to the Sacred Mountain in the Black Hills into a great cave, where he sat with select wise men of the earth, as a pupil of Maiyun (the Great Spirit). Maiyun gave four sacred arrows to Sweet Medicine with instructions for sacred use.

There is a great mystery around the Sacred Arrow Bundle. Arrows caused animals to be confused and to be killed, also to turn back and defeat enemies. Arrows killed them and made their horses run off. The Arrow Keeper said sacred prayers. Medicine men sang sacred songs.

59

#15 Cheyenne Warrior
Courtesy of Azusa Publishing, L.L.C.

#16. Chief Two Moons
Cheyenne War Chief
Courtesy of Azusa Publishing Company, LLC

#17 Treaty Indians
Courtesy of Azusa Publishing, L.L.C.

#18 Cheyenne Girl & Doll
Courtesy of Azusa Publishing, L.L.C.

#19. Cheyenne Chiefs Little Wolf & Dull Knife
Courtesy of Azusa Publishing, L.L.C.

The Cheyenne, like many Plains Indians, observed the Sun Dance ritual. They built the Sun Lodge and cut the sun pole to use as the center pole in the actual Sun Dance. Warriors were suspended from the center pole and hoisted in the air by pegs inserted into slits in the chest.

The dance went on all night and warriors tried to rip the pegs from their chests during the dance. The Sun Dance was the most popular ceremony and represented world renewal. They pledged to the Sun God for a sick friend or for safe return from battle.

The introduction of the horse to the Cheyenne, circa 1760 brought much change. They acquired the horse and quickly became a buffalo hunting society. Millions of buffalo roamed the plains and they quickly adapted, as horse mounted buffalo hunters. The Cheyenne became great breeders of horses and established trade centers for commerce with other tribes.

The Cheyenne pushed west to the Black Hills in the early 1800's, and began a relationship with the Oglala Sioux. The Sioux had allies in the Northern Cheyenne and Arapaho, but the Crow were their enemies. Circa 1830, Cheyenne Indians divided into the Northern and Southern Cheyenne.

The Northern Cheyenne dwelled on the Great Plains in western Montana, Northwestern Nebraska and eastern Wyoming. Then in 1825, the Cheyenne and the white man signed a friendship treaty. After 1830, they lodged near Bent's Fort, in southern Colorado.

In 1863, Southern Arapaho, Southern Cheyenne, Comanche, and Kiowa attacks closed the Santa Fe Trail and there was full scale war on the Great Plains. The Cavalry fought the hostile Northern Arapaho, Cheyenne, and Lakota and in pursuit, the Indians often fired the prairie to detain them.

#20 Kicking Bear, Minneconjou Sioux
Courtesy of Azusa Publishing, L.L.C.

The Arapaho were Plains Indians closely bonded to the Cheyenne and ranged in the same territory of eastern Colorado and Wyoming Territory. They both spoke Algonquian, but the dialect varied so much that one could not understand the other so both tribes kept their own languages. The Arapaho were so mellow that other tribes called them, "Blue Sky People." The Arapaho Confederacy was divided into the Northern Arapaho and the Southern Arapaho Indians. Arapaho, Nebraska was named after the tribe.

The Cheyenne band packed up and broke camp. The band of usually 150-300 Indians followed the bison. The whole camp moved behind the bison herd as it migrated, while the horse pulled the travois and toted large loads of teepees, camp gear and even infants. Buffalo utility made many implements for the Cheyenne: robes, saddles, shields, tipi skins and other items. The buffalo was the main supplement of the Plains Indians.

The Cheyenne were notorious for being eaters of puppy meat. Other Indian tribes found it disgusting; some just mused about it. It was the same with horses. Some Indian tribes ate horse meat, while others balked.

Cheyenne Dog Soldiers in the 18th century were fierce warriors, who wore black sashes and swore to fight the enemy. The first soldier rode ahead, dismounted and anchored himself with his lance thrust through the black sash into the ground to protect his comrades and they would die if necessary.

In 1865, Arapaho, Cheyenne and Lakota raided settlements up and down the North and South Platte Rivers. Chief Roman Nose wanted revenge for Sand Creek and led several hundred Cheyenne braves against the Cole and Walker columns marching to Fort Laramie in late September, 1865. They harassed the troops for several days, until Conner's other column arrived.

At dawn, on November 25, 1876, Colonel Rand MacKenzie led 600 cavalry and 400 Pawnee Indian scouts in an attack on Chief Dull Knife's sleeping Cheyenne village, on the Red Forks of the Powder River by Crazy Woman Creek near the Bighorn Mountains. Indians fled the village under fire, but forty died, including Dull Knife's son and son-in-law.

Chief Dull Knife led his band to the 1876-1877 winter camp of Oglala Chief Crazy Horse, who surrendered with his band the following spring at Fort Robinson, Nebraska. They later were transferred to Fort Reno. An act was passed in Congress to relocate the Northern Cheyenne to Indian Territory.

May 28, 1877, 937 of Dull Knife and Little Wolf's (photo, pg 64) Cheyennes started on the long trek to Indian Territory. The Cheyenne traveled along the well worn Texas Cattle Trail on their journey and arrived at the Arapaho and Cheyenne Agency.

They hated it there and were unwilling to take up farming. Dull Knife's Cheyenne suffered starvation there. Many of their children died and within a year, they left the agency taking the same route northward. These hostile Indians fought with U.S. Army units and killed 40 male settlers in Kansas.

Reaching Nebraska, Chiefs Dull Knife and Little Wolf's bands split off. Dull Knife, again led his people to the Fort Robinson and Red Cloud Agency, where they were incarcerated in an old military barracks.

That night, with little heat, food and water, the band tore up the floor of the building and escaped, but that was a mistake because soldiers fired at them as they fled for their lives. In all, 22 males, eight females and two children were slain. Dull Knife lost a daughter and granddaughter.

In 1880, the government outlawed the Sun Dance, a holy ritual of the Plains Indians in order to assimilate the Indian into American culture.

Chapter Four
DAKOTA WAR

In 1860, the Sioux population in America was 30,000. In 1862, Congress passed the Homestead Act that made land belonging to various tribes of Indians accessible to non-Indian settlers. This was the beginning of migration to Indian lands for settlement.

Prospectors discovered gold along the Upper Missouri River in 1862. Numerous gold miners flocked to the area. Before long, five to six hundred miners had passed through Fort Benton on the way to the gold fields.

On May 27, 1862, Agent Samuel Latta reached Fort Pierre by steamboat. Three thousand friendly Brule, Hunkpapa, Minneconjou, Sans Arc, Two Kettle, and Yanktonai Sioux lodged in the valley. These were reservation Indians, at peace with the white man, willing to receive annual annuities.

Agent Latta had arrived with presents for the chiefs and annual annuities. He held a feast on board ship for the chiefs that night. Sitting Bull was there, as was Chief Old Bear Rib, a peace chief.

The next day, Latta made a speech about keeping the peace with the white people. Old Bear Rib and twelve other chiefs gave speeches about remaining peaceable. His band moved out to hunt buffalo on the Little Missouri on June 5th. The Chief and his band had planned to rejoin later.

One hundred fifty hostile Minneconjou and Sans Arc Sioux arrived to trade at Fort Pierre. They wanted to know where the peace chiefs were and bragged that they would kill them. Word from the hostiles reached the lodge of the old Chief. The next day he showed no fear and appeared inside of the stockade and was approached by two Sans Arcs, Mouse and One-That-Limps. Mouse shot Old Bear Rib at close range, hitting him in the chest. Old Bear Rib shot them both with his double barrel shot gun, and killed them, as he died.

The Santee Sioux having crop failure, faced starvation in 1862 and that winter the government allotment didn't reach them. They had their fill of palefaces in their territory. The white-eyes did not go away. Instead more and more appeared on the horizon. Little Crow led the Dakota War of 1862. Santee Indians warred on the Minnesota settlers and killed over 1,000 people.

Merchants stopped credit for food to the Santee people; war broke out on August 7, 1862, when discontented braves killed a farmer and most of his family. Fervor spread as more attacks occurred on the Minnesota River.

The Santee attacked a trading post and killed Andrew Myrick, the owner. Myrick heard that the Indians were starving and publicly made a statement to the effect that if the Indians were hungry, "let them eat grass." He was found dead on the floor of his store, his mouth stuffed full of grass.

In August, the Dakota Sioux attacked the settlers on the Minnesota River near their reservation, killing hundreds of white people. An Army was recruited and formed under Brigadier General Henry Hastings Sibley, a veteran Indian trader, who was the first governor of the state of Minnesota.

The Santee had gone on the warpath in August of 1862. Sibley led his forces up the Minnesota River Valley and pitted his recruits against the rebelling Sioux and won a victory on September 22, 1862, at the Battle of Wood Lake, defeating the Dakotas in Minnesota. The U.S. Army captured 1,700 Santee Sioux and marched them to their fort.

Three hundred three Santee Sioux were tried and found guilty of murder and rape of hundreds of settlers and sentenced to be hanged. President Lincoln commuted the sentences of 284 Sioux warriors and signed off on the execution by hanging of 38 Sioux warriors in the town of Mankato, Minnesota on December 26, 1862. It was the largest mass execution in American history.

In the aftermath, the government suspended annuities to the Dakota for a period of four years and extended the money to victims of the raids. The 284 offenders were imprisoned in Iowa, where half of them perished.

As the Santee Uprising came to an end, Little Crow left the region. Minnesota had passed a law giving $25.00 for every Sioux scalp. While Little Crow and his son stopped to pick berries, settlers opened fire on the Indians, mortally wounding Little Crow, on July 3, 1863. His scalp was publicly displayed and his son was later captured in Dakota Territory.

During the summer of 1863, approximately 5,000 Bluecoats arrived to contain the Sioux. General Sibley joined General Sully to fight the Lakota Indians. The hostility between them was mounting. Sully headed up the Missouri River, while Sibley rode northwest out of Minnesota.

Brigadier General Sibley led his troops from Fort Ridgely, Minnesota in pursuit of the Santee warriors into the Dakotas. Sibley's forces marched all day on July 24, 1963, when his scouts reported seeing a Sioux camp of many lodges a few miles off. Sibley ordered them to bivouac near a salt lake and had his men dig in. As they made camp a number of friendly Sioux approached the scouts on the edge of camp and began to talk.

Army surgeon Josiah S. Weiser joined them and began to converse, when a Sioux warrior cut him down with his rifle and fled.

#21. Katie Robideaux, Rosebud Sioux
Courtesy of Azusa Publishing, L.L.C.

More warriors, who were waiting in ambush, attacked. Sibley's men met the assault by charging across the ravine, approaching Big Mound. They attempted to dislodge the Sioux braves, who were firing at them. Cavalry, Infantry and artillery fire routed the Sioux, who fled in disarray onto the prairie in broken terrain. A running battle ensued that day, as ordered. The soldiers returned to camp at nightfall, some returning the following morning. The Battle of Big Mound left the Sioux band beaten and broken.

Sibley had attacked the Dakotas in Minnesota. After a major battle with Sibley's forces, the Eastern Dakotas fled southward and reached a Lakota hunting camp at Big Mound on July 24, 1863. Santee and Teton Sioux had combined forces. They joined the Dakota to fight General Sibley's Army in the Battle of Dead Buffalo Lake on July 26, 1863 and the Battle of Stony Lake on July 26, 1863. General Sibley's cavalry and artillery caused the Sioux warriors to retreat in the direction of the Missouri River.

The Sioux crossed the Missouri and disbanded. It is not known if Sitting Bull fought in these battles. Sitting Bull chose to keep their lands and wanted the white man leave. General Sibley and his troops returned to Minnesota, while General Sully and his complement traveled to Fort Pierre.

On September 3, 1863, Major House and a complement of 300 men under General Alfred Sully, aided by the Second Nebraska Company under Major Peaman, who was in charge of a wagon train, two Companies of Iowa Sixth under the command of Major Ten Broeck and a battery (two or more big guns) of the Iowa Fifth, under Captain A. J. Millard, attacked a Sioux Indian village of 1,200 Blackfeet, Hunkpapa and Yanktonai Sioux at Whitestone Hill in North Dakota. The soldiers surrounded the village and were ordered to dismount and fight until the enemy broke. They took command of the hills on the perimeter and formed a line and commenced firing.

There was little resistance, while others just turned and ran, making it across the Missouri River. About 120 Sioux under Chief Little Soldier surrendered. There were men, women and children captives with ponies and domestic dogs. Sully had the soldiers build bonfires and the buglers blow "rally" in order to have them all assemble.

The morning of the 4th, the men searched the hillsides looking for Indians. The Army scouts fought a skirmish or so, and discovered one hundred bodies and several horses that were killed. General Sully burned 300 tipis, goods and buffalo meat which had been stored in skins.

General Sully led nearly 3,000 U.S. Army soldiers and accompanied a wagon train and moved toward the Knife River. Several thousand Sioux warriors had assembled under Chief Sitting Bull and Chief Four Horns. Sitting Bull's nephew, White Bull, was also present.

The encampment stretched over three miles along the Badlands of the Little Missouri River. Sully's Winnebago scouts fought 30 Sioux braves, while riding ahead of the Army column, July 26, 1864.

On a hot day on July 28, 1864, the Battle of Killdeer Mountain took place in North Dakota. Sully's scouts came in and reported having seen about 1,400 Dakota Sioux lodges in the Killdeer Mountains. An equation for the population of an Indian camp was figured by the Army using five members per lodge and fourteen hundred lodges equaled approximately 7,000 Indians. Sully left the wagon train at the Heart River with several hundred troops to guard them.

General Sully commanded 2,200 U.S. Army troops and several batteries of artillery. General Sully arranged the Army in the "phalanx" formation (a hollow square formation by soldiers). Inside of the square were ambulances, transport wagons, two batteries and command staff; every fourth cavalryman held the reins and walked four horses, inside of the phalanx.

In 1862, during the Powder River War, Crazy Horse had been the outstanding Sioux war chief in battle. The warriors began to paint their bodies and their horses in preparation or war. As White Bull watered his horses, Sioux Indian scouts warned him of oncoming troops. Chiefs Four Horns, Sitting Bull, and White Bull rode with several hundred Sioux warriors.

Horse-mounted Sioux warriors in red war-paint sat watching the soldiers. As they came within five miles of their camp, a Hunkpapa warrior named, Lone Dog rode out and taunted the soldiers and warned that if he was shot, all of the Sioux would commence firing. He explained that White Bull was a ghost and hard to hit. Bullets started to fly, and Lone Dog retreated.

Five miles from the village at the foot of the Killdeer Mountains, the battle began. The Indians and soldiers fought in close combat. The Sioux charged toward them in waves, as they struck and withdrew, using only bow and arrows and outdated muskets for fire.

The hills were dry and without vegetation and the hillsides were too broken for normal cavalry maneuvers. Much of the cavalry dismounted for action, firing Spencer rifles. About every five miles, the Sioux fired at the soldiers along shallow valleys and low ridges, as they neared the village. Arrows and lead flew. Warriors on horseback flanked them on both sides and the rear. Sully sent artillery back to disperse them.

Chief Inkpaduta's Sioux warriors attacked Sully's column from the right side. A Minnesota battalion drew sabers and charged them. The Indians held their ground. Many Indian died under artillery fire and from the Spencer rifles. As the fighting got heavy, the soldiers dismounted and issued intense fire from there carbines. Two soldiers and 27 Indians died in the fray.

In the midst of battle, a warrior walked out leading a horse pulling a travois; a middle aged man lay on it, named Man-Who-Never-Walked, who wished to die. Flying bullets killed the horse and the invalid. He got his wish.

Sitting Bull, riding his sorrel, led the Sioux in battle and fought courageously;. His uncle, Four Horns was shot in the back; Sitting Bull rode to his uncle's side, grabbed his horse's reins and led him to safety. The battle ended and the Sioux exited into the hills. The Indians suffered over 100 casualties and lost their food supply at Killdeer Mountain. Sully's firepower was superior and finally the Sioux retreated to the Badlands. Two soldiers were dead, and ten wounded, but General Sully had the victory!

Sully ordered 700 men to destroy tents and goods. Sixteen hundred lodges were torched along with tons of buffalo meat and piles of hides. They shot all the abandoned dogs. July 29, 1864, they returned to Heart River.

The fleeing Sioux had set up camp at the head of the Heart River. They were reinforced by more Brule, Minneconjou and Sans Arc Sioux and endeavored to attack Sully's column, supply wagons and the wagon train, but were held back by his artillery.

The procession slowly moved through the gorges, steep trails and narrow passages, yet their only weapons were their bow and arrows and spent muskets; their food supply was gone and they were becoming quite gaunt.

From August 7-9, 1864, at the foot of the Killdeer Mountains hundreds of warriors, amassed to fight General Sully's forces during the Cheyenne-Sioux Wars in the Missouri Badlands. On August 8, 1864, during the Battle of the Missouri Badlands, one of Sully's Winnebago Indian scouts struck up an open exchange in the dark of the night with Chief Sitting Bull.

"We are thirsty to death and want to know what Indians are you?" Sitting Bull said, "Hunkpapa, Sans Arc, Yanktonai. Who are you?"

"Some Indians with the soldiers." came the reply, with one Indian badly shot through the arm. "The soldiers are hungry and thirsty," he added, "so just stay around and they will be dead."

Sitting Bull shouted back. "Why did you come with the soldiers? You have no business with the soldiers." he declared. "The Indians here have no fight with the whites. Why is it that the whites come to fight with the Indians?" Then he said, "We have to kill you and dry to the earth."

On July 9, 1864, the wagons had traveled through the deserted Sioux camp, slowly moving out of the Badlands toward the Plains. The Sioux warriors crossed the Little Missouri River and scattered.

Sitting Bull led bands of Sioux on the trail of a buffalo herd in late August of 1864, when they encountered the Fisk emigrant wagon train of 150 pioneers headed on a low divide between the Grand River and the Badlands, guarded by Captain James L. Fisk, who was commissioned to open land routes to the mining fields in the Black Hills.

Fisk and 50 enlisted men accompanied the Fisk wagon train. The Sioux warriors shadowed the wagon train awaiting an opportunity for them to attack.

On September 2, 1864, the men attempted to cut back the bank to allow passage down the steep slope to Deep Creek. As they attempted the descent, the first wagon overturned and another pulled over to the side. Three emigrants with nine soldiers stopped to upend it.

The wagon train moved up about a mile, when Sitting Bull and about 100 Sioux ambushed the emigrants. Riding fast, Sitting Bull wrestled with a soldier mounted on his horse; the soldier pulled his pistol and shot the Chief. The ball passed through his left hip and out through the small of his back.Sitting Bull shifted to the opposite side of his horse and rode off under cover.

Jumping Bull and White Bull rode to his side, held him on his horse and managed to lead the Chief to safety. They helped him down, bandaged his wounds and assisted Sitting Bull back to the village, some six miles distant. Sitting Bull was not among his warriors for the rest of the fight.

The Sioux ambush took them by surprise. Hand to hand combat with the warriors wielding knives and tomahawks, with their bow and arrows, cut back the number of emigrants and soldiers, while the wagons continued to roll slowly forward at a snail's pace for three days.

On the third day, they circled the wagons and managed to hold the Indians off, with the use of a howitzer. Six soldiers and two teamsters were killed. Three emigrants vanished.

In another wagon attack by the Oglala band along the Platte River, a white woman, named Fannie Kelly was captured and traded to a Hunkpapa Sioux, named Brings Plenty. She was held hostage and forced by the Sioux to write a ransom note using the nose of a lead bullet delivered to the Fisk wagon circle which the emigrants had made into a barricade and named it Fort Dilts.

#22. Brule Chief Hollow-Horn-Bear
Courtesy of Azusa Publishing, L.L.C.

The whites first saw Mrs. Kelly through field glasses, intending to trade. Fisk offered coffee, flour, sugar and three horses for the release of the captive, but the Sioux wanted four wagons loaded with food and did not relent, but hung around waiting them out. Curriers left and brought help from the Missouri region. Soldiers escorted the emigrants to safety.

Young Chief Bear Rib arrived at Fort Sully with two hundred Blackfeet and Hunkpapa Sioux warriors and parleyed with Capt. John H. Pell, Adjutant General to General Sully. Young Bear Rib said it was bad to wage war. Captain Pell told him more forts would come and they must bring in the female captive. Six chiefs vowed to try. The chiefs from Fort Sully offered horses in trade for his captive, but Brings Plenty refused to release her.

Mrs. Kelly was held captive four months, when Sitting Bull intervened. He went to Brings Plenty's tent and demanded the captive from him. The Sioux gave her the name, "Real Woman." Sitting Bull personally escorted the hostage to Fort Sully and turned her over to the Army saying, "She looked homesick, so I took her back." The Sioux left on a buffalo hunt.

The Military prevented the Indians from trading for firearms at the military forts, but Gall and Sitting Bull traded for guns at Fort Berthold, instead. Sitting Bull often camped near the fort and served as an emissary between the French fur fort and the Sioux and always brought a gift for Frederic Gerard (the proprietor) every time he visited the fort, who never reciprocated. Sitting Bull bartered with them for two years, and quit because Gerard did not pay him the agreed price. Sitting Bull admired a black stallion, owned by Gerard. The horse was one that Gerard rode as a scout for Custer at the Little Bighorn. Sitting

Bull merely mounted the horse and rode off, saying, "Now, I have one of the horses Gerard owes me."

General Sully had led his troops on a mission to wipe out the Sioux. They rode in and routed them from their winter camps, burned their lodges and food supplies and killed their horses. General Sully erected Fort Berthold and Fort Union deep in Sioux territory and built Fort Rice on the west bank of the Missouri manned with soldiers. General Sully had twice defeated the Sioux, destroyed their villages, supplies and buffalo meat.

A band of Cheyenne and Lakota attacked Julesburg, Colorado in January 7, 1865. On June 14, 1865, peaceful Indians rebelled at Horse Creek.

The Battle of the Platte River Bridge occurred on July 24-26, 1865. A platoon of cavalrymen was ordered to meet a wagon train in the Powder River country. A Sioux and Cheyenne Indian war party killed all of the cavalry and wagon drivers and escorts, near the Platte River Bridge.

July, 1865, General Conner left Fort Platte, leading three columns, and launched a military campaign against the Sioux in Powder River country. He received the order to attack and kill every male Indian over age twelve.

Fort Rice was erected on a grassy low area surrounded by low hills and the Missouri River on the east. The palisade structure were built of cottonwood logs in Sioux territory, heckling Lakotas raided the fort regularly.

Friendly Hunkpapa under Young Chief Bear Rib and Two Bear's Yanktonai pitched their teepees near the fort and helped defend it until Sand Creek, when 130 lodges abandoned the fort.

April 14, 1865, Lincoln was assassinated, as the war was drawing to a close. President Jackson was busy during the reconstruction period.

81

Soldiers were ordered to the Western front, as many deserted and ran to avoid fighting the Indians. Having seen enough fighting, many Blue-coats just wanted to return home. Confederate prisoners were given the choice of fighting Indians or rotting in a Union prison.

July 28, 1865, Sitting Bull led 300 warriors in revenge for the massacres by the military. The battle began as he rode, clad in full length headdress, loin cloth and moccasins, followed by six horse warriors, adorned in red war paint, and rode for two of the trader's horses. Reins in hand, Sitting Bull spurred his favorite pony, Bloated Jaw, in retreat. The braves surrounded the fort and stole livestock around the perimeter. They charged using hit-and-run tactics and were driven back and fought with knives and tomahawks.

Sully used his artillery to shell groups of warriors, while sharpshooters fired at Indian targets from the walls. The sniper fire continued, but when the sun was directly overhead, the Sioux had withdrawn. One soldier was killed and four men had arrow wounds in the Battle of Fort Rice. He called on Sitting Bull to surrender. Sitting Bull slashed his limbs. He was in no position to surrender at this time and would never concede his people's homeland. His refusal blocked the peace process.

General Conner continued his campaign against the Sioux in the Powder River country; Conner's column destroyed an Arapaho village. The Army burned buffalo meat, tents and robes. Two columns, two thousand strong, under Lt. Col.. Samuel Walker and Col. Nelson Cole joined forces north of the Black Hills in North Dakota and crossed the hot plains, as the animals began to give out in August of 1865. The soldiers were near collapse as they moved along the Powder River toward the Yellowstone River.

On the first of September, 1865, the detachment marched along the Powder River. Crazy Horse led a mixed band of Sioux Indian braves in an attack on Cole's column which lasted three days. The column's Spencer carbines held them back, but they shot some soldiers and gained a few horses.

The temperature was the biggest enemy. On September 3, 1865, 225 horses and mules died of the heat. The soldiers abandoned many supply wagons. "A" Company charged the Indians.

September 5, 1865, a Sioux war chief wearing only a loin cloth and moccasins rode out adorned in red war paint, with two feathers in his hair. He carried his buffalo skin war shield, rifle, bow and arrows; Sitting Bull sat on his sorrel horse, Bloated Jaw. The Chief was accompanied by Black Moon, Jumping Bull, and White Bull, Bull Eagle, Bull Head, and Stand-Looking-Back, who rode in among the cavalry and killed four with their rifles.

The eighth and tenth of September, the relentless Crazy Horse struck again. Ahead lay the village of Little Wolf's Cheyenne and Red Cloud's Oglalas. The Hunkpapa sent word to Red Cloud of approaching soldiers.

October 1865, General Conner left two Companies at Fort Laramie, one they had constructed, on the fork of Crazy Woman Creek and the Powder River. Oglala Chief Red Cloud surrounded the fort and kept it isolated during the winter of 1865-1866, soldiers died of malnutrition. Relief came when Colonel Carrington's company arrived June 28, 1866.

John M. Bozeman blazed a trail that split off the Oregon Trail, in eastern Wyoming Territory northwest of Fort Laramie between the North Platte River and Montana Territory gold mines and cut through the Sioux buffalo hunting grounds in Montana and Wyoming Territory.

#23 Oglala Sioux Chief Red Cloud
Courtesy of Azusa Publishing, L.L.C.

Chapter Five
RED CLOUD'S WAR

In April of 1866, Cheyenne Chief Dull Knife and Sioux Chiefs Red Cloud, Spotted Tail and Standing Elk, and other chiefs met at Fort Laramie to discuss the use of the Powder River country with the government and conducted talks to negotiate treaties with the Sioux.

While they talked, Colonel Henry Carrington and 700 hundred infantrymen reached Fort Laramie with the intention of building forts in Sioux territory on the Bozeman Trail. Carrington led his troop column into the fort. The Army invaded the Powder River area of north-central Wyoming Territory.

Chief Red Cloud became angry and spoke, "The Great Father sends us presents and wants us to sell him the road, but the white chief goes with soldiers to steal the road before the Indians could say yes or no." The angry chief prophesied of Carrington and his troops in their land, "In two moons, the command will not have a hoof left." He led his warriors from the peace table in June of 1866, infuriated, which incited him to go on the warpath.

Red Cloud declared war on the whites after the U.S. Army purposely built the forts in the Powder River Valley on his tribe's hunting grounds. His Oglala went on the war path in the Powder River Valley and in Colorado and Wyoming at the same time. Red Cloud's War, also called the Powder River Valley War exploded in 1866 over control of the Powder River country and the Bozeman Trail, also known as the Bozeman War. Chief Red Cloud waged war against the three soldier forts and miners along the Bozeman Trail and the Powder River, which cut through Sioux hunting grounds.

When the U.S. government attempted to take the sacred Black Hills from the Sioux Nation after gold was discovered, troops were sent in to enforce the law. Red Cloud, who boasted 80 coups as a Sioux warrior, and his Oglala warriors went to war early in 1866 and initiated the most successful Indian War ever waged by an American Indian Nation against the U.S. Army.

Colonel Carrington chose the spot to build the fort on the Sioux's favorite hunting grounds. Soldiers felled large trees in order to build the stockade Fort Phil Kearny, which served as his temporary headquarters.

Early in autumn Red Cloud returned to the Powder River country; his scouts reported that the *"wasichus,"* (white man) had advanced 200 miles from Fort Laramie to the Big Piney on the Bozeman Trail in Sioux territory.

Red Cloud summoned scattered bands of Arapaho, Cheyenne, and Sioux Indians to assemble for a council after completion of their annual bison hunts. As the Indians arrived, the Arapaho, Cheyenne, Crow and Lakota chose to harass the soldiers at Fort Phil Kearny after it was built. They made a series of raids using hit and run tactics versus direct attacks. A crew of Carrington's woodcutters working northwest of the fort was attacked by a Sioux war party. Captain Fetterman's small band of cavalry came to their rescue, but rode into an ambush that left two soldiers dead and some wounded.

Colonel Carrington sent two companies 90 miles to the northwest to build another outpost on the Bozeman trail. A different fort, called Fort Reno which had been built two years earlier, was fortified to continue service.

August of 1866, the Hunkpapa Sioux war parties began raids on Fort Buford. Sitting Bull captured the saw mill and ice house. The Sioux fired at the fort. Sully answered fire with artillery and drove them off.

#24 Red Cloud Delegation to Washington
Photo taken in Omaha, Nebraska in 1875
Courtesy of Azusa Publishing, L.L.C.

#25 Red Cloud, Oglala Chief of Red Cloud's War
Courtesy of Azusa Publishing, L.L.C.

\# 26 Aging Sioux Chief Red Cloud
Courtesy of Azusa Publishing, L.L.C.

#27 Jack Red Cloud, Son of Chief Red Cloud
Courtesy of Azusa Publishing, L.L.C.

#28. Red Cloud's Bedroom
Courtesy of Azusa Publishing, L.L.C.

The next day, the Sioux returned and held the same stronghold. Sitting Bull taunted the soldiers inside Fort Buford. Indians set their supply of firewood ablaze. Artillery fire cut down two Sioux warriors. The infantry stormed the ice house and saw mill. They rode off toward Fort Union.

Sitting Bull approached the fort waving a white flag and asked to speak with David Pease, the chief trader. Pease had some provisions set outside. The chief demanded a red shirt or they would kill everyone in the fort. Pease obliged. All of the soldiers at Fort Buford were advised to direct fire on the red shirt that Sitting Bull was wearing. The Hunkpapa Sioux held the fort in isolation throughout the whole winter. The citizenry thought the worst: that the Indians had destroyed all of the occupants of Fort Buford.

Carrington requested reinforcements and in November of 1866 received one company of cavalrymen and a group of officers. One officer was Captain William J. Fetterman, a Civil War veteran.

There was talk among Fetterman's men bragging that they should go out and take Red Cloud's scalp. Captain Fetterman stationed at an outpost in the Powder River Country, once boasted, "Give me 80 men, and I'll ride through the whole Sioux nation."

Four thousand warriors arrived along the Tongue River by December. The assembly was only a day's ride from Fort Phil Kearny. Colonel Carrington did not picture the threat that was there from the powerful Sioux.

With the success of the raid on Fort Phil Kearny, Red Cloud sent one of his lieutenants, Chief Crazy Horse to strike them again. Crazy Horse led a war party of Oglala warriors against the Long Knives. One of Crazy Horse's favorite tricks was the decoy maneuver.

On December 21, 1866, U.S. Army Captain Fetterman and 80 Cavalrymen streaked out of Fort Phil Kearney on horseback in pursuit of Crazy Horse and his Sioux war party. Crazy Horse and nine other warriors rode ahead of them as decoys down to the valley floor below where thousands of braves lay in ambush. Fetterman and all 80 cavalrymen were massacred in the trap. As help arrived, they saw the wild Indians ride off in the distance.

The autumn of 1867, the Arapaho, Cheyenne, Comanche, Kiowa and Plains Apache Indians signed the Medicine Lodge Treaty of 1867. Some famous chiefs that signed were Black Kettle, Brave Man, Satank, Satanta, Spotted Wolf and Ten Bears. Chiefs Crazy Horse, Red Cloud and Sitting Bull were in attendance. Comanche Chief Quanah did not attend.

Crazy Horse's Oglala fought the pale faces August 1, 1867, in the Hayfield Fight. He struck again the next day at the Box Wagon Fight, during Red Cloud's War.

In 1867, Lieutenant Colonel Custer was transferred out West to head the 7th Cavalry (photo, pg. 120). He had been a young illustrious officer, who gained rank in the Union Army during the Civil War, who they called the "Boy General."

Although Custer was requested to bring the Cheyenne and Sioux Indian tribes onto the reservations, he ignored the orders. In 1868, Custer attacked the Cheyenne Indian people at the Battle of Washita, massacring the whole village. Custer was the type of flamboyant officer, who wore a bright red kerchief around his neck into battle and expected to be accompanied by a brass band. He blatantly murdered the Indians.

In 1868, the Nez Perce Indian Treaty, resolved the Nez Perce War. It was signed and ratified, the final treaty ratified in America by Congress.

Chief Crazy Horse rode with American Horse, Little-Big-Man (photo, pg 142) and other Sioux, on a raid attacking Horseshoe Station, March 19, 1868. Fetterman's Outpost, on the Bozeman Trail and Elliot's Squadron, on the Wichita River in 1868 had been wiped out by Comanche attacks. Frustrated, General Sherman ordered that his officers should wipe out as many Indian camps as possible to reduce their numbers as Red Cloud's War raged.

The Laramie Treaty of 1868 divided the Teton Sioux into two groups: the reservation Indians and the hostile or non-treaty Indians dwelling in the Powder River country led by Hunkpapa Sioux Chief Sitting Bull.

Surprisingly enough, Chief Red Cloud had won the War of Powder River Valley (Red Cloud's War); the only Indian war won by the American Indians. His prediction had come true. Despite the Army's efforts to keep the supply road open, Chief Red Cloud had closed the Bozeman's Trail, Fort C.F. Smith, Fort Phil Kearny, and Fort Reno in 1868.

Sioux chiefs remained unwilling to sell the Black Hills, but Red Cloud came into Fort Laramie with other chiefs in 1868 to end the Powder River War and signed "The Treaty of Laramie" on November 6, 1868 and relinquished the Black Hills, closed the Bozeman Trail, created the Great Sioux Reservation and was given the perimeters for the reserve at Rosebud and let the Sioux keep their hunting grounds in Montana and Wyoming.

The Army abandoned the three forts on the Bozeman Trail and as they withdrew their garrisons, Red Cloud ceased to make war. The treaty ended the Dakota Wars and the Sioux agreed to remain at peace. The Sioux were given presents and expected to live by farming versus hunting bison. Congress gave them rations for subsistence, while converting to agriculture.

Father De Smet administered to many different tribes, including the Sioux, for over thirty years. He had returned to his home in St. Louis, when the Second Treaty of Fort Laramie Council was formed. Father De Smet was contacted and he sojourned to Fort Laramie for the council. Peace was established between the U.S. Army and the Lakota Sioux Nation.

The council was opened as the Indians danced and sang. Four Horns lit the peace pipe and offered the smoke to the four directions, mother earth and the sun. The head chief spoke to the Council asking Black Robe to speak with ears open to hear. Black Robes words were well received. The Sioux greatly admired the holy man. Sitting Bull exhibited true Sioux hospitality and insisted that Black Robe stay in his lodge as his guest.

As mapped out in the 1868 Treaty of Fort Laramie, Sioux Territory was reduced to Heart River in North Dakota in the north and the Platte River (in Nebraska) in the south and the Bighorn Mountains in the west to the east side of the Missouri River, including the western half of South Dakota.

Red Cloud was a Sioux statesman, yet some Sioux thought that he was overly ambitious. Sioux chiefs Red Cloud, Crazy Horse and Sitting Bull were divided over warring with the U.S. Army. Red Cloud wanted peace. Crazy Horse and Sitting Bull wanted war. Sitting Bull wanted the white-eyes off their lands and did everything in his power to drive them off. After the Laramie Treaty, the Lakota continued on the war trail raiding in Montana, Nebraska and Wyoming. The Sioux hunting reserve stretched between the Black Hills and the Bighorn Mountains, north of the Platte River.

Chief Black Kettle moved his people to a new village in 1868, on the Washita River in Oklahoma. Four years after the Sand Creek

Massacre at dawn on November 22, 1868, George Armstrong Custer led his Long Knives to ambush Black Kettle's peaceful village, known as the Washita Massacre.

Chief Black Kettle and his wife rode out to meet the army. They displayed a flag of truce, but Custer's troops shot them down in cold blood. The elderly men, women and children were either shot or trampled by the soldier's horses. The flamboyant Custer, a drunkard, boasted of winning the Indian battle. Arrogant Custer was loathed by the Indians and many officers.

Lt. Colonel Custer noticed an attractive Cheyenne woman, named Monahseta among the captives, at Washita. He was married, but took her for a mistress. She shared Custer's tent with him for the next four months, until he joined his wife at Fort Hays. She gave birth to a fair, yellow haired baby boy named, Montoete, for Armstrong in Cheyenne, after Custer.

In 1868, the government provided the Wind River reservation for Chief Washakie's Eastern Shoshoni as a reward for always being peaceable to white settlers, soldiers and trappers. The reserve covered three million acres in Wyoming's Wind River Valley.

1869, the First Sioux War ended and the treaty was signed by the U.S. Army and the Sioux Indians at Fort Laramie.

On January 23, 1870, 100 Plains Blackfeet were massacred by the U.S. Army on the Marias River in response to the murder of Malcomb Clark.

In 1870, the U.S. government forced the Arikara, Hidatsa and Mandan Indians to live on the Fort Berthold Reservation in Dakota Territory. The 15th Amendment, March 30, 1870 gave Americans, including Indians, the right to vote, which was ratified by Congress. However, women, considered a minority, could not vote.

Red Cloud traveled to Washington D.C.in 1870 to meet with the "Great White Father" and lost the trust of many of the Sioux people. In 1871, he and a fraction of his Dakota people moved to the Red Cloud Agency in Nebraska. Red Cloud busied himself as emissary between the red man and the white man as a peace-chief during the Black Hills War.

On March 3, 1871, Indian tribes lost the right to have sovereign nations through treaties. Instead, they became wards of the state. March 17, 1871, Kiowa chiefs Big Tree, Satank and Satanta led the attack on a wagon train in Texas. Chief Satank was killed as he left the scene. Big Tree and Satanta were freed of the crime of the Warren Wagon raid.

Satanta was jailed later for a raid that he did not commit; he was on a buffalo hunt at the time and was wrongly convicted. He committed suicide in prison.

Sitting Bull had the duty to lead his hunters to kill 30,000 buffalo annually to feed his whole tribe, but in 1871 the government sponsored programs for wholesale slaughter of the buffalo on the Plains in order to force the Indians onto the reservations. Ten thousand white hide hunters amassed on the Great Plains, killing millions of buffalo, took the hides, ate the tongues, and left the carcasses to rot. The days of the buffalo were numbered.

Spotted Eagle's band joined other Lakotas and formed a village of 2,000 lodges on the bend of the Powder River. After their sun dance the Lakota planned to war against the Crow, and penetrated Crow country in the Yellowstone Valley. Scouts reported seeing an Army camp north of the river.

Baker's command escorted a party of 20 railroad employees and had established a base camp on the Yellowstone. August 11, 1872, the Sioux grouped in the timber, across the river. Heavy fire broke and

#29 Spotted Eagle, Sans Arc Sioux
Courtesy of Azusa Publishing, L.L.C.

lasted all day. Warriors crossed the wide river to assault the troops in the Battle of the Yellowstone.

Sitting Bull and White Bull observed the fighting from the higher elevations. As the battle wound down, Sioux marksmen fired on the soldier camp, across the Yellowstone River. The fighting soon came to an end.

Baker's company bivouacked opposite the mouth of Arrow Creek on August 12, 1872. They camped on a bank of the river in the loop. The next night, the Sioux held council to decide whether to engage the Army or fight the Crow. Meanwhile, parties of young ambitious braves slipped past the Akicita (police) out of camp, initiating the Battle of Arrow Creek.

White Bull proceeded toward the soldier camp and encountered Crawler and two other Brule comrades leading stolen stock from the soldier camp, as fire broke out. The Hunkpapa returned fire, as Plenty Lice was shot dead and fell off of his horse. His body was thrown onto a campfire.

Council ended, deciding war with the soldiers was eminent. At sun up, the warriors assembled facing the enemy camp; soldiers found shelter and dug in. They initiated their assault on the soldier's camp, but were driven back. Warriors fired from the heights, as Crazy Horse and Sitting Bull looked on. Warriors taunted the soldiers by racing back and forth, emitting war-cries, and firing shots at the camp, daring the Army to fight them.

Sitting Bull walked from his teepee in full view of the soldiers with his rifle, bow and quiver of arrows. He wore his loin cloth, leggings, war shirt and moccasins, with two feathers in his hair. Sitting Bull sat cross-legged and held a pipe in his hand and invited other Indians to join him in a "smoke." Calmly, Chief Sitting Bull filled his pipe from his tobacco pouch.

White Bull, Gets-the-Best-Of and two Cheyenne seated themselves in a circle with the chief. The pipe was lit and later, White Bull called it a "smoking party." Chief Sitting Bull sat and smoked and passed the pipe, as bullets whizzed around them hitting the dirt, their hearts pounded.

Sitting Bull smoked until the pipe was out, tapped out the tobacco and returned the pipe to his pouch; he rose and walked slowly out of sight. The others jumped up and ran off, but White Bull had to return for his bow and arrows. Sitting Bull gained acclaim from his people for his bravery by his smoking exhibition.

The chief insisted that they stop the antics, but Crazy Horse wanted to ride the daring line again and asked White Bull to join him. Crazy Horse wore a white shirt, loin cloth and moccasins, hair down with two feathers; he chose the lance and rode the line. A bullet killed his horse. He ran for cover.

The Baker expedition's engineers refused to proceed down the Yellowstone. Instead, they insisted on reaching the safety of Fort Ellis.

Chief Gall (photo, pg 111) was Sitting Bull's lieutenant and ranked second to Crazy Horse in valor as war chief and was an excellent leader in battle. Gall led attacks on U.S. Army troops along the Yellowstone in 1872-1873.

Gall had seen the Long Knives' advance on their village. Taking cover in some trees, he and his war party delivered fire on their encampment. Twenty Hunkpapas raced toward some stock, corralled in by wagons and tents, the infantry blocked their advance, as they rode through the camp. Stanley tried to signal Baker with cannon fire, about the Indians.

Chief Gall attacked Major Baker and Col. Stanley's complements intermittently, causing them to take cover. An engineer from Baker's group wandered into the hills hunting agates and was accosted by the Indians. The others mounted up and exchanged rifle fire with the Indians, rescued the man.

Finally, Gall walked down to the river's edge and laid down his rifle, announcing that he wanted to speak to the soldier chief. Stanley did the same and strode to the opposite bank. Gall refused to meet him halfway on a sandbar, but they attempted a conversation through an interpreter.

Gall wanted to know what soldiers were doing in Sioux country and asked how they planned to pay for the lands used for building the "iron horse" (railroads). He threatened to bring hundreds of Indians to fight them. When numerous curious warriors gathered behind him, Stanley retreated.

An exchange of fire began and the soldiers returned fire, killing two Indians. Sitting Bull arrived with his band of Hunkpapas, on the evening of August 21, 1872.

The next morning, the Sioux attacked the soldier camp from the rear, warriors fired from the bluffs. Wagons were corralled and the infantry formed a perimeter around them. Stanley sent two companies to dislodge the Sioux on the bluffs. Sitting Bull gave an oratory threatening the soldiers and rail workers if the railroad came through. The Battle of O'Fallon's Creek ended.

As the Army column moved across the Little Missouri Badlands and down the Heart River, Sioux warriors followed and attacked them from the shadows with hit-and-run tactics making random forays on the soldiers.

On the Yellowstone, Custer and Stanley's columns joined. There were nearly 400 lodges of Minneconjou and Hunkpapa Sioux situated in harm's way of the oncoming columns. Having gotten word of the approaching Bluecoats, the Sioux packed their goods in buffalo-skin bull-boats and swam their horses across the Yellowstone. The U.S. Army arrived on the bank of the river; August 10; the soldiers failed to make it across the fast flowing river.

Sitting Bull, along with Cheyenne braves, Minneconjou, Oglala, Sans Arc, and Hunkpapa Sioux warriors left a huge encampment on the lower Little Bighorn River and arrived the following day on the Yellowstone River.

The next day, the column moved out along the Yellowstone and turned north at the Musselshell River. The Sioux headed south up the Bighorn, but a few Indians stayed around and watched the column disappear from sight.

General Sherman vowed to Congress to protect the railroad workers from Indian attack in America in March of 1873 and sent George Armstrong Custer and the 7th Cavalry to defend them.

In 1873, Custer had a chance encounter with Crazy Horse and Sitting Bull, while guarding the surveyors for the Northern Pacific Railroad on the northwestern plains. Crazy Horse fought Stanley, an officer under Custer's command on August 11, 1873.

June 27, 1874, Comanche Chief Quanah Parker formed his war party of allies of some 700 Arapaho, Cheyenne, Comanche and Kiowa braves and rode to Adobe Walls to attack the "paleface" buffalo hunters a mile from the ruins of the old Adobe Walls site where the Comanche fought Kit Carson.

Quanah led the war party, as they swarmed down on Adobe Walls harboring twenty three buffalo hunters, holed up in the fort. The thunder of hoof-beats, rifle cracks and war whoops filled the air.

One hundred yards out on the first charge, a bullet from a buffalo hunter's long-rifle shot Chief Quanah's horse out from under him. At that point, a second bullet hit the Chief. The Indians carbines were no match for the buffalo hunter's Sharps rifles. A bullet struck the medicine man's horse right between the eyes.

The attack called the Red River War was a loss. Only four buffalo hunters died, while nine Indians were killed. The Indians retreated. The Comanche fought over laws passed to exterminate the buffalo. It was "The Last Plains Indian War." Some called it "The Buffalo War" instead.

On September 10, 1874, a band of Comanche and Kiowa Indians assaulted an Army caravan along the Washakie River in Indian Territory. They held out during several days of attack until reinforcements arrived, one died.

In 1874, Lt. Col. Custer violated the 1868 Laramie Treaty and led his 7th Cavalry, 1,200 civilians, geologists, miners, newspaper men, and 100 wagons into the Black Hills and found rich land suitable for farming and gold.

The government removed the Sioux to allow miners into the Black Hills. They arrived by the thousands with the gold rush and broke the existing Laramie treaty with the Indians. Custer blazed the "Freedom Trail," to the Black Hills, but the Lakota Indians called it the "Thieves Road."

In 1875, General Miles attacked a band of Cheyenne Indians near McClellan Creek. The Comanche Indians were facing starvation during the winter of 1875 with the removal of the buffalo and many surrendered. Nearly 8,000 hostile Cheyenne and Sioux Indians surrendered from 1871 to 1881.

The Comanche had resisted the white man's intrusion since 1840 and fought a long fight with the Texas Rangers, called the Texas-Indian War. Two hundred Quahada had signed the Treaty of Medicine Lodge. Now Quanah Parker and 400 Comanche Indians surrendered on June 2, 1875, at the same time driving 500 horses into Fort Sill, Oklahoma.

#30. Sioux Encampment on the Little Bighorn
Courtesy of Azusa Publishing, L.L.C.

General MacKenzie assaulted five villages and massacred women and children, burned their villages to the ground in Duro Canyon, and ordered 1400 horses destroyed in 1875; the troops played havoc with the Comanche.

In 1875, the Red Cloud Delegation visited President Grant in Washington D.C. Chiefs Red Cloud, Sitting Bull, Spotted Tail, and Swift Bear of the Sioux Nation all attended. President Grant met with the Sioux Indian chiefs in Washington to discuss the sale of the Black Hills and Powder River country, but it wound up in failure. The Sioux, in response, initiated the Second Sioux Indian War.

The Sioux and Arikara Indians traded horses and held horse races. A fight broke out and both tribes took hostages. Finally, Sitting Bull and the Arikara chief came to an agreement and returned the hostages. Sitting Bull came away riding a beautiful stallion and wearing an eagle feather war bonnet.

Dakota, Lakota and Yanktonai Sioux were camped along the Grand, Heart and Lower Yellowstone Rivers poised for war. Three Sioux warriors set a trap and an army scout blundered into the ambush and lost his life just as the Cavalry arrived. In return, they killed the Indians and carried their heads on poles, (much like scalp poles) and placed them on a hill as a warning to the Sioux. Crazy Horse, Sitting Bull and other Sioux fought the gold miners who swarmed over Sioux territory of their Black hills in 1875. Crazy Horse was emboldened with the courage of the people and was a brave and daring leader.

In 1875, angry over the settlers and miners occupying their lands, Oglala Sioux Chief Red Cloud demanded that the U.S. government abide by the rules of the 1868 Treaty of Fort Laramie and leave their sacred Black Hills. Despite efforts from the Sioux, the white man continued to occupy their land.

#31. Sioux Squaws on Horses
Courtesy of Azusa Publishing, L.L.C.

Chapter Six
BLACK HILLS WAR

A law was passed in Congress that all Indians report to agencies on reservations by January 31, 1876 or be considered hostile. The Sioux Indians were given the ultimatum, but they were not informed of the order until after the deadline. In 1876, the hostile Sioux, Cheyenne, and Arapaho Indians joined forces in Montana and went on the war path.

The Sioux Indian Nation declared war on the American U.S. Army. The action that ensued was called the Great Sioux War of 1876-1877 or the Black Hills War and was made up of several major battles between the U.S. Army and the Lakota Sioux fought in the Powder River Country. The Sioux word for their sacred Black Hills was "Paha Sapa." In 1876, the Sioux Nation was ordered to the Rosebud Reservation in South Dakota. Many thousands of "Reservation Indians" remained at the Agencies during the Great Sioux War of 1876.

On February 7, 1876, the Secretary of the Interior announced that it was past time and the Sioux were now considered hostiles, saying it was now a military matter and authorized General Philip Sheridan to begin operations against hostile Sioux, including chiefs Crazy Horse, and Sitting Bull.

On March 16, 1876, Brigadier General Crook moved his troops north from Fort Fetterman in Wyoming through the Powder River Valley. The Indians called General Crook "Three Stars," the same number of stars that were on his uniform. Finding an Indian trail, Crook deployed Colonel Reynolds and six men to scout for their village.

At dawn March 17, 1876, Crook's dragoons led by Colonel Reynolds, who believed it to be the camp of Crazy Horse, assaulted the Cheyenne-Sioux encampment of He Dog and Two Moons on the Powder River and drove the Indians into the hills. The Sioux returned fire from the bluffs. Many Indians were killed. Reynolds captured all of their horses and set fire to their lodges. Some fled to the camp of Crazy Horse, who helped push the Long Knives back and the cavalry made a hasty retreat. In a night raid, the Cheyenne and Sioux recaptured all of their stolen ponies. Crook reunited his forces, but in blizzard conditions and short of supplies, and retreated to Fort Fetterman.

General Crook embarked from Fort Walla-Walla to engage the Indians in the Black Hills War, June 17, 1876. Shoshoni Indians fell in to the rear of Crook's column to give battle to their old enemy, the Sioux. Crook deemed the Sioux to be the best American Indian cavalry he had ever seen.

Crook's column quietly approached and surprised the camp of Crazy Horse, who rallied his 1,200 warriors and drove General Crook back. Crook retreated in the Battle of Rosebud Creek, eight days before Custer entered the Little Bighorn Country.

Three days before the Battle of the Little Bighorn, the Teton Sioux held their annual Sun Dance. Chief Sitting Bull performed in the ritual. He vowed to have 50 strips of skin, cut from each arm, as sacrifice to the gods, a type of self mutilation.

Sitting Bull began the feat midday and danced all night until the sun was overhead the following day, while warriors mutilated themselves. Sitting Bull passed out from loss of blood and had a vision. They threw water in his face to revive him. When he gained consciousness, the chief spoke.

In his vision the holy man saw many long knives (U.S. Army soldiers) descending on them like grasshoppers. In his dream, the Blue coats (U.S. Cavalry) fell down on the ground in defeat and the Sioux Nation was the victor!

~~~~~~~

Sitting Bull's dream caused him to prophesy to the Sioux council that their warriors would deliver a great blow to the blue-coats. Sitting Bull had gathered the largest army of Indians ever assembled on the Columbia Plateau.

Hostile Sioux bands gathered at the Little Bighorn numbered two thousand Arapaho, Blackfoot-Sioux, Brule, Cheyenne, Hunkpapa, Minneconjou, Oglala, and Yanktonia Sioux Indian warriors. Sitting Bull, Crazy Horse, Gall, Red Cloud, and Spotted Tail poised to attack. They called Custer, "Long or Yellow Hair." He and Sitting Bull were pitted as rivals in that campaign.

Without Custer's knowledge, the largest band of American Indian warriors ever assembled amassed under Chief Sitting Bull at the Great Sioux Reservation in Rosebud, South Dakota. The Arapaho, Cheyenne and Sioux warriors numbered 2,000 strong. Sitting Bull was chief of the entire Sioux nation; no other Sioux chief attained as much in war, politics and religion.

Kicking Bear fought at the Little Bighorn. Kicking Bear and Red Feather, the brother in law of Crazy Horse were supposed to have killed Little Brave, one of Custer's scouts from the 7th Cavalry, but Arikara scout Red Bear said that he had found the Custer scout wounded on the east bank of the river.

#32 War Chief Sitting Bull
Courtesy of Azusa Publishing, L.L.C.

#33 First War Chief Gall
Adopted Brother of Sitting Bull
Courtesy of Azusa Publishing, L.L.C.

#34. "Sitting Bull"
Great Oglala Sioux Indian Chief
Courtesy of Azusa Publishing, L.L.C.

#35. Crow King, Hunkpapa Sioux Chief
Courtesy of Azusa Publishing, L.L.C.

#36. Chief Rain-in–the-Face
Courtesy of Azusa Publishing, L.L.C.

Lt. Colonel George Armstrong Custer was a famous figure in the old west and the Civil War. He was ranked high in the Union Army at an early age and had attained the rank of General. George married Elizabeth "Libbie" Bacon (photo pg. 118) and was stationed out West to lead the 7th Cavalry; she dined with him in the field. His brother Tom and nephew, Boston rode in his ranks. Custer's was promoted to brigadier general in 1863 and because of the stars on his uniform, Indians called him "Son of the Morning Star."

On June 25, 1876, George Armstrong Custer led five companies of his 7th Cavalry in hot pursuit of the Sioux Indians along the Little Bighorn River. Custer made a fatal mistake by dividing his companies into three groups.

At the Little Bighorn, Custer led two companies, while Major Marcus A. Reno (photo pg. 121) took two companies and Captain Fredrick Benteen, (photo pg. 122) took one company of men to Glen Creek, then rode along the east side of the river. Benteen stayed close and if he saw no Indians, was to return to ranks.

An egotist, Custer wanted the glory and was in denial about any impending disaster and disregarded the huge number of Sioux gathered there. Instead, he was over confident over his own strength in the field.

Custer's Crow Indian scouts (photo pg. 124) informed him that there were too many Indians. The cocky Custer was so conceited that he would not listen to their advise. The Crow Indian scouts changed out of their army uniforms on the Little Bighorn and into their own Indian garb and prepared to die, knowing their fate. When questioned by Custer, they told him that they were prepared to die in their native garb. The general became outraged and dismissed his Indian scouts. This may have been a drunken rage.

#37. Curly, Crow Indian Scout for Custer
Courtesy of Azusa Publishing, L.L.C.

#38. Lt. Col. George "Longhair" Custer
Courtesy of Azusa Publishing, L.L.C.

#39 Mrs. George Custer
Courtesy of Azusa Publishing, L.L.C.

#40. Tom Custer, Brother of George Armstrong Custer
Courtesy of Azusa Publishing, L.L.C.

#41. Custer's 7th Cavalry Gathering
Courtesy of Azusa Publishing, L.L.C.

#42. Major Marcus A. Reno
Courtesy of Azusa Publishing, L.L.C.

#43. Captain Fredrick Benteen
Courtesy of Azusa Publishing, L.L.C.

#44. "Custer's Last Stand"
Courtesy of Azusa Publishing, L.L.C.

#45. Custer's Crow Scouts at Battlefield
Courtesy of Azusa Publishing, L.L.C.

Meanwhile, Chief Sitting Bull orchestrated the positions of his chiefs, Crazy Horse, Crow King, Gall, Red Cloud, and Spotted Tail, who were poised for attack. Gall was military chief of the Hunkpapa Sioux Indians. He served as war chief under Sitting Bull and was his lieutenant. Gall was admired as a fighting warrior. Gall led raids on the "Blue-coats" along the Yellowstone in 1872 and 1873 and was a brilliant warrior and Sioux war-chief.

The Battle of the Little Bighorn was fought on June 25, 1876. The temperature was fast approaching triple digits as Custer's three companies rode hard charging Chief Sitting Bull's village. Custer and Reno's offensive approached both ends of the Rosebud Sioux village.

Custer attacked the Sioux village with two companies. Major Marcus A. Reno took two companies and Captain Fredrick Benteen led one company of men to southwest Glen Creek, then rode along the east side of the river. Captain Benteen stayed close and seeing no Indians, returned to ranks.

Reno attacked the other end of the village. While in combat, Reno needed help and Benteen rallied to his defense. In the attack, Gall lost two wives and three children to Reno's forces in the village. Chief Gall seeing his family killed took out his rage on Major Reno and forced him to retreat.

War chief Gall then turned his wrath on Custer at "Greasy Grass." He led the assault and joined Chief Crazy Horse, meeting Custer's forces head on, with a frontal attack with hundreds of Sioux warriors. General Custer's battalion literally fought for their lives that day. Crazy Horse gained fame on June 25, 1876, at the Little Bighorn fighting General Custer. Crazy Horse was the greatest Sioux warrior ever recorded. Custer was portrayed to be a great hero by back-east newspapers, but was actually a coward.

Sioux Chief Rain-in-the-Face (photo, pg 114) suffered humiliation being arrested by Captain Tom Custer (Little Hair), (pg. 119) brother of Lt.Colonel George Armstrong Custer and swore that someday he would cut out his heart.

Two years later, Rain-in-the-Face got his chance to make good his vow at Greasy Grass. He sang the war-song; as he smelled the acrid, blue grey smoke of battle, his anger rose. The Chief showed no fear wearing his sacred white weasel tail; he felt invincible. Mindlessly, the chief rushed in and grasped the Bluecoats' flag. His pony was shot out from under him; he used his tomahawk on the flagman and ran back to his ranks with the flag.

The Chief caught and mounted another pony, espied "Little Hair" and spurred his steed toward him, killing Bluecoats as he rode. Closing in on Tom Custer, he saw fear in his face and shot him with his revolver. Rain-in-the-Face remounted his pony and rode off, gratified, but sick of war. Whether Tom Custer's body was mutilated is not known. Rain-in-the-Face denied it.

Greatly outnumbered, Custer's 7th Cavalry fought on. Surrounded by Indians, Lt. Colonel Custer and two hundred and ten men fought to the death. The Cheyenne Indians remembered "Long Hair" from his massacre of Chief Black Kettle's village and hated him with a passion.

The Sioux took no prisoners. The Indians' numbers were too great; Custer and all of his men were killed that fateful day. Reno's army, reinforced by Benteen's command had many losses yet lived to fight another day.

Forty eight hours after the battle was over, Colonel Gibbon's column, with Terry's Headquarters staff and the Dakota Infantry column reached Reno and Benteen; they accompanied them out of hostile territory. Colonel Gibbon led his column, turning east as they scouted for any Indians to engage.

The battle is referred to as Custer's Last Stand, or the Battle of the Little Bighorn. Chief Sitting Bull's dream had come true. The soldiers had fallen like grasshoppers. The Sioux had their revenge!

After the battle ended, the warriors did the Victory Dance in celebration. Sioux war chiefs Gall and Crazy Horse were credited with the victory over the 7th Cavalry at the Battle of the Little Bighorn in the Black Hills War. Crow King played a major role in the battle.

Custer died on June 25, 1876. When his mistress Monahseta saw the body, she told the warriors to leave it alone. Monahseta took a bone awl and pierced Custer's ears, so that he could hear better in the spirit world.

Crazy Horse attacked Sibley's scouts on July 7, 1876. The Sioux said Custer must not have heard the chiefs when they said if you break the land peace promise, you will surely die. A statue of Custer on his horse was erected near his old hometown in Monroe, Michigan.

After Custer's defeat, Red Cloud was distrusted by the white man and accused of aiding the Sioux. He was made to resign as the chief of his Agency and moved his band to Pine Ridge, but had to resign as chief there. He agreed to the reduction of the Sioux Reservation size and lost popularity.

After the Battle of the Little Bighorn, some Lakota scattered into Canada, while others found refuge on other reservations. Crook feared the Reservation Indians would leave and join the warring Cheyenne and Sioux.

Crook had orders to locate the war-camps of the Cheyenne and Sioux. He believed the encampments of Crazy Horse and Sitting Bull to be located on the headwaters of the Powder, Rosebud and Tongue Rivers in Montana Territory.

In 1876, the Battle of War Bonnet Creek, during the Black Hills War, was fought three weeks after the Battle of the Little Bighorn. The Army knew that 1,000 Cheyenne warriors had left the Red Cloud and Spotted Tail Agencies to join the hostile Sioux encamped at War Bonnet Creek. The U.S. Cavalry attacked them there and forced them back onto the reservation.

The Army planned to block the supply route between the Powder River Country in Wyoming and the Red Cloud and the Spotted Tail Agencies in Nebraska. On July 17, 1876, the Fifth U.S. Army Cavalry, under Colonel Wesley Merit engaged the Cheyenne Indians in battle near the Red Cloud Agency on northwestern Nebraska and southeastern Montana.

One of the scouts in the fight was William F. Cody, later known as "Buffalo Bill." Will also worked as a scout for George Armstrong Custer, fought the Sioux Indians and admired them for their courage. While on patrol, he led a company into battle with hostile Cheyenne Indians.

During the battle, Cody shot the horse out from beneath a Cheyenne war chief, named Yellow Hand in a duel; his second shot killed the chief. He then held up his scalp and war bonnet and claimed the first scalp for Custer. Cody bragged of his accomplishment after the fight. The account of Cody's fight with Chief Yellow appeared in the New York Herald.

Colonel Nelson A. Miles embarked by paddleboat up the Missouri River to the Yellowstone with the Fifth Cavalry leaving Fort Leavenworth, Kansas late summer to help contain the uprising Cheyenne and Sioux, after their major victory over George Armstrong Custer and the 7th Cavalry (photo, pg 120).

General Phil Sheridan disbanded the Dakota column and left the area. Colonel Miles joined Brigadier General Terry on the Rosebud in autumn; the combined forces moved up the Rosebud River from Yankton, South Dakota to reconnoiter with Crook and crossed the Tongue River to their destination. General Crook's forces had pursued the Sioux for 300 miles from southeastern Montana and had run low on supplies. The men had resorted to eating horseflesh.

Crook sent Captain Anson Mills to obtain rations. Miles and Terry's forces split from General Crook at the Powder River. Miles and Terry reached Glendive, Montana Territory on the Yellowstone River, where the troops established winter headquarters on the mouth of the Tongue River.

On September 9, 1876, General Crook engaged the Sioux in September in the Battle of Slim Buttes, 70 miles north of the Black Hills, during the Black Hills War. Crook connected with General Terry, briefly and moved out on his own. Crook and an army of 2,000 soldiers encountered a camp of 250-300 Minneconjou and Oglala Sioux Indians. The Indians drove the cavalry and infantry back, before reinforcements arrived and destroyed the village and ran off most of the Sioux. Crook's outfit ran short on food and the column turned south, on what became known as "Starvation March."

Once, a band of Oglala Sioux from Crazy Horse's camp nearby, rode in to intervene, but disbanded when they saw too many soldiers. The Indians' supplies, skins and tipis were destroyed, but large amounts of buffalo meat were salvaged for their consumption, since their food supplies were low.

While Colonel Elwell S. Otis and his troops escorted a wagon train of 100 wagons from Glendive to supply Colonel Miles, the Sioux attacked the slow moving wagon train traveling along Spring Creek, on October 11, 1876. During the skirmish, several mules were killed and the Indians temporarily drove off some of their wagons. Otis pushed to reach Miles, but the Sioux again attacked the wagons on October 15, on Spring Creek. The detachment held off the Indians and continued on.

Two Sioux emissaries spoke to Otis and suggested that Colonel Miles meet with Chief Sitting Bull. Miles agreed and at Sitting Bull's request, Miles met with the Chief, north of the Yellowstone River at Cedar Creek on October 20th. In their discussion, Sitting Bull proposed a trade for ammunition to hunt buffalo. He gave his word that they would not use it to harm the soldiers, if left alone. Miles informed the Chief of the Army's terms for surrender. Neither Miles, nor Sitting Bull were pleased, but agreed to meet the next day.

Chief Sitting Bull met with his minor chiefs and some of them wanted to return to the reservation. Sitting Bull swore he would kill any chief trying to go back. Many of his chiefs wanted war. On October 21, 1876, Miles and Sitting Bull resumed talks. The chief made demands on Colonel Miles that the soldiers leave and that no wagon trains would be allowed in Sioux country. The talks were going nowhere. Miles and Sitting Bull returned to their camps.

The Sioux began firing on the soldiers and a skirmish erupted. Chief Sitting Bull retreated. The Army claimed to have chased the Indians over 40 miles. In their haste, the Indians dropped various supplies and left their spent Indian ponies. The Army pursued and on October 27, 1876, more than 400 lodges of 2,000 Sioux people, including Red Cloud and Spotted Tail, surrendered to Colonel Nelson A. Miles and peacefully returned to their reservations. Others fled toward Canada, pursued by Colonel Miles' forces. The battle that was fought became known as the Battle of Cedar Creek, fought in Montana Territory in the Black Hills War.

On December 7, 1876, Baldwin and his command proceeded along the Missouri River toward the Milk River in Montana, before dawn and marched his men right past Sitting Bull's camp. His adopted brother, Jumping Badger, rode among the troops and Baldwin thought he was one of his scouts.

Jumping Badger reported to Sitting Bull and the Hunkpapa fled across the ice of the frozen Missouri, with 600 warriors, willing to spring the trap on the Bluecoats.

The Hunkpapa Sioux fired across the river and the Long Knives returned fire. A "norther" blew in that night and the soldiers nearly froze in their knapsacks. They marched back to Fort Peck in the morning. General Crook shut down his operations because of blizzard conditions.

On December 16, five chiefs journeyed to the mouth of the Tongue River to meet for talks with "Bear Coat" Miles at the soldier fort. Instead, Miles' Crow Indian scouts shot them down as they neared the fort.

Sitting Bull had collected as much ammunition as he could at the request of Chief Crazy Horse. He had stored up quite a surplus of ammo and was leaving to rendezvous with Crazy Horse.

Sitting Bull with about 120 Sioux lodges trekked southeast toward the Red Water, between the Missouri and the Yellowstone. Chief Sitting Bull chose a campsite below some bluffs near the mouth of the Red Water east of Ash Creek.

Anxious to overtake Sitting Bull, Baldwin used wagons pulled by mules to haul his troops to Red Water. They reached Sitting Bull's camp on December 18, 1876. The Hunkpapa saw the soldiers approaching and sent their families south ahead of them to safety.

Baldwin captured Sitting Bull's abandoned camp. He salvaged what he needed and burned the rest. There were lodges, buffalo meat, horses, mules and utensils, a devastating loss to Sitting Bull. Baldwin's men took advantage of hundreds of warm buffalo robes, in the dead of winter.

Sitting Bull and the Hunkpapa fled leaving their lodges, meat supply and horses, which was a great loss to them. Their lodges went up in smoke, as did the stored buffalo meat for the winter. Baldwin headed down the Yellowstone and joined Miles and his command at the Tongue River post.

The U.S. government introduced the Sell or Starve Bill (the Agreement of 1877) in order to force the Lakota Sioux to sell their sacred Black Hills. The Lakota people suffered, but refused to sell.

Miles' favorite climate to fight Indians was during winter. Harsh weather created poor conditions for them to fight, with food being scarce. The colonel used this technique to his advantage; his men had heavy clothing.

Miles had followed Sioux Chief Crazy Horse and Cheyenne Chief Two Moons for the previous ten days. Miles' 5th column had been recently increased by several companies to 1,000 men. As dawn broke in the Wolf Mountains surrounding the Tongue River Valley, on January 7, 1877, Miles' scouts rode hard into camp to report that a number of hostile Indians had amassed about a quarter mile from camp. Using his binoculars, Colonel Miles could see hundreds of Cheyenne and Sioux Indians and deployed his men.

After a two and one half mile march, Miles ordered a bivouac and sent his Crow scouts out to reconnoiter if any Indians were near. They returned after a few hours with nine Northern Cheyenne women and children who had been wandering in search of Crazy Horse. Head Scout, "Yellowstone Kelly" reported to Colonel Miles of the capture one and one half miles away.

In the meantime, a party of Cheyenne-Sioux had been close by when Miles' scouts captured the Cheyenne women and children. Not knowing of any contact by Big Horse and thinking the captives were in danger, the Indian party had set a trap. A few Indians, as decoys, began to walk around in the snow feigning to search for something.

Back at camp, Crow scouts reported seeing Indians walking around where they had taken captives in the hills to the south. Yellowstone Kelly, Tom Leforge, George Johnson, James Parker and John "Liver-Eating" Johnston rode in hot pursuit of the Indians, hoping to take prisoners. Thinking they had ridden unobserved, Kelly drew out his rifle and fired as they rode pell-mell toward the Cheyenne decoys.

As they narrowed the gap between them, 40 or 50 warriors appeared from the trees, firing at them. Two of the scouts' horses were shot out from under them and a bullet grazed Johnston's head, parting his hair. Miles' scouts rode for cover behind fallen trees and boulders and were pinned down. Hearing the rifle reports, the soldiers in camp formed a circle surrounding the perimeter.

Colonel Miles ordered Captain James S. Casey, A Company, 5th Infantry and a field artillery unit and Lieutenant E. Hargous and his company to the aid of the scouts in the Battle of Wolf Mountain.

One hundred Cheyenne and Sioux had amassed by then. Relief fire from smaller caliber weapons continued for over an hour, but artillery fire from the big gun drove the warriors into the hills.

They had no knowledge that Big Horse, a Northern Cheyenne, had escaped capture. On January 7, 1877, after a long journey through the snow hunting for Crazy Horse and Two Moon's camp, Big Horse finally reached Crazy Horse's encampment.

Big Horse gave a wolf call, a howl, as a greeting. He supplied them with all of the news of the capture and warned them of Miles' location. Hearing this, the Cheyenne and Sioux prepared for the war trail. The Indian warriors readily prepared for war: painting their faces, bodies and their horses.

Crazy Horse, Two Moons and their bands started down the Tongue River. The combined bands of Cheyenne and Sioux followed the Tongue River until they were close to the soldier camp. The two bands split up and planned to strike Miles' forces from two directions.

Two Moons and the Cheyenne would attack from the south, while Crazy Horse and the Lakota, stayed along the Tongue River and would attack from the west hoping to draw the soldiers into an ambush.

Colonel Miles had made bivouac in a bend of the Tongue River on level ground. He had chosen a defensible spot. "Bear Coat" Miles suspected another attack on their camp from the west and moved E Company, 5th Infantry to Battle Butte and also moved Carter's K Company 5th Infantry into the trees.

During the night, Indian sharpshooters dispersed rifle fire into the soldier camp. Unaware of the failed decoy ploy, Big Crow and his warriors, in heavy falling snow, split up from Crazy Horse and Medicine Bear's war parties.. The Cheyenne and Sioux war parties advanced during the night toward the soldier camp.

The bugler sounded reveille at 4:00 a.m., the morning of January 8, 1877, Miles sent out scouts to look for any Indian activity in three feet of snow. The scouts rode back in a hurry, reporting Indian movement.

The Colonel mounted his horse and rode to the plateau, where E Company had bivouacked for the night and gazed through his binoculars, as Crazy Horse's war party tried to hide from view; others formed a firing line, very close to K Company. Ewers observed Medicine Bears line of braves riding toward them and positioned his men along the plateau. They directed fire at the approaching Indians, as did Pope, with artillery guns.

As Chief Medicine Bear rode along the Tongue River, he displayed a talisman that he believed had much power. Its purpose was to protect him and draw fire. He believed that bullets couldn't hurt him and that the talisman would protect his band as they crossed into the hills, south of the army.

The Cheyenne crossed the bare area with few casualties, but an artillery shell struck Medicine Bear's pony knocking both horse and rider to the ground. Luckily for the old chief, the shell did not detonate; shaken, Chief Medicine Bear rode toward the hills.

The Cheyenne warriors held a vital position and pinned down the infantry men using rapid fire. The outcome of the battle was pivotal, now at this point. Failure would jeopardize the whole outfit. Ewers repositioned his men to the north side of the plateau.

The warriors closed in on the soldiers fighting in the valley adjacent to the butte south of Ewers, as other Indians crossed the river. Yellowstone Kelly informed Miles that warriors had gathered on three ridges southeast of the plateau. This gave the Indians good position overlooking them.

Colonel Miles moved A Company into the hills across the valley and pulled C and D Companies from reserve onto the plateau. As Casey led A Company across the valley in deep snow, Medicine Bear's band began firing at them. Casey's company made the first two hills, as the fighting slowed. Miles, seeing the pause, sent D Company to assist and fortify the position. Lieutenant McDonald led D Company across the valley floor and ascended the slope parallel to D Company.

A number of Indians joined Medicine Bear on the third ridge. Big Crow, a Northern Cheyenne shaman, dressed in red and wearing a full length war bonnet, danced in front of the soldiers, unafraid. He believed that his powers were strong and that bullets could not hurt him. Bullets flew around Big Crow. Two soldiers from D Company, below him fired at the medicine man. A bullet brought him down, lowering the Cheyenne's morale.

Sitting Bull arrived at Crazy Horse's village situated at the mouth of Prairie Dog Creek at the Tongue River and delivered the ammunition that he had requested on January 15, 1877 with about 100 remaining lodges. Many hunting bands assembled led by chiefs Black Moccasin, Black Shield, Lame Deer, Little-Big-Man, No Neck, Red Bear, Spotted Eagle and White Bull. In December, peace chiefs were a majority.

The chief circled from the north through the open plain to the east. A few Cheyenne braves deserted, but Big Crow's medicine did not affect Crazy Horse's Sioux. The shrill screech sounds coming from eagle bone whistles filled the air. The Sioux chief was brazen enough to attack two Companies of at once. Crazy Horse advanced, leading 300 warriors within 50 yards of MacDonald's Company, as the Indians fired on them.

Colonel Miles deployed C Company to reinforce A and D Companies. Butler marched his men across the valley. Halfway across, the Indians fired a volley of rounds at them, while other warriors attacked McDonald's position.

Miles barked an order to Lieutenant Baldwin to redirect Butler to take the third hill and drive the Indians back. Butler led C Company up the hill on horse back when an Indian's bullet shot his mount out from under him; Butler climbed the hill on foot. With Butler badly in need of ammunition, Lieutenant Baldwin's company raced across the ice and up the mountain with the munitions.

Indians remained on the second and third ridge. Hundreds of soldiers and Indians battled that day. Warriors under Crazy Horse were forced back onto the summit of the third hill, but the Sioux held on and fired with Sharps and Winchester rifles in rapid succession; their aim was far from accurate.

Knowing the Sioux's strength, Miles ordered Pope to lay down artillery fire over the Army's heads and shell the Indians. Heavy fire from the Rodman gun and Napoleon cannon drove the warriors back down into the valley.

Weary and nearly out of ammo, Butler called off the advance, as heavy snow fell. Crazy Horse, the Cheyenne and Sioux Indians were in full retreat as the Army pursued them, firing. Crazy Horse and his band retreated.

Miles posted guards as lookouts, in case the Indians returned and warned the troops to be on alert, with Companies stationed at strategic points.

Inside of five hours, the Battle of Wolf Mountain in the Black Hills War was over and Colonel Miles had the victory. They spent the

#46. Crazy Horse's Friend, Touch–the-Clouds
Courtesy of Azusa Publishing, L.L.C.

rest of the day inspecting the field of battle. Dead Indian ponies lay all around. The hostiles had tied lassoes around their dead comrade's bodies and used their horses to drag them off.

On the sixth day of May in 1877, Crazy Horse, Little-Big-Man, and Little Hawk with their bands surrendered at the Red Cloud Agency near present day Chadron, Nebraska. Crazy Horse and 1,000 Oglala Sioux sang war songs and brandished weapons as they entered Fort Robinson. They herded 12,000 horses to the fort, and surrendered 117 firearms.

Miles led his troops from the Tongue River Fort and defeated the Sioux, ending the Black Hills War with the Teton Indians. One of the Army's final battles with the Sioux Indians was fought on Lame Deer Battlefield on Muddy Creek, a tributary of the Rosebud River, on May 7, 1877.

Miles' troops ambushed Chief Lame Deer's Minneconjou, surprising them. The chief began to surrender, but a fight broke out between Chief Lame Deer, his son, twelve warriors and four soldiers; some of them were killed. Forty five hundred Minneconjou surrendered and agreed to move onto the reservation. Many tribes surrendered to Miles, but the Brule and Oglala Sioux had resisted capture.

In 1877, the Nez Perce Indians were forced into war by the U.S. Army. Around 800 Nez Perce Indian warriors, under Chief Joseph, retreated and eluded the Army and fought a running battle on horseback for over 1,500 miles. Joseph's fighting tactics were brilliant, often outsmarting the Army. The Nez Perce were captured about 40 miles from the Canadian border. Had he no had his whole village in is care, Joseph could have made Canada.

The irony was that Nez Perce Chief White Bird and his band of followers escaped during the peace talks and successfully made it into

Canada. Joseph's fighting Nez Perce would have made it into Canada, also, had they not been slowed by women, children and about 2,000 horses and camp utility.

Chief Joseph and the Nez Perce tribe had one favorite breed of horse, the Appaloosa, one type of horse brought from Spain. When Joseph surrendered, thousands of horses were confiscated and taken from the tribe; some of these were killed, but enough were saved to continue the species.

Crazy Horse walked across the prairie and came upon a dead eagle. He returned to his lodge and cried out sadly, that he had seen his own dead body lying on the plains. He had foreseen his own death.

A night or two later, Crazy Horse had a dream. *He dreamed and saw himself riding a magnificent white stallion.* The medicine man had always believed that no bullet could ever kill him because he had powerful medicine.

There was uneasiness in the camp of Crazy Horse on the Little Cottonwood. Rumors were rampant about Crazy Horse reuniting the Oglala to return to war. His friend, He Dog warned him of impending trouble. The Army frowned on the Sioux hunting buffalo, to make things worse.

Crazy Horse again dreamed. *A spotted eagle flew high over the bluffs, north of Red Cloud, but plunged to the earth at the dreamer's feet. It had a steel knife stuck deep in its wing. Blood filled the eagle's moccasin, beaded with the zigzag of lightning.*

A rumor was started by a Sioux scout, named Woman's Dress, which was not true. The plot was told that Crazy Horse planned to council with General "Three Stars" Crook. The story was at the time that they were to shake hands, Crazy Horse planned to kill the soldier chief, but it was a lie. "Three Stars" Crook offered a reward of $100.00 and a sorrel horse for Crazy Horse and issued an order to take Crazy Horse to Fort Robinson. Out of fear, many turned against the chief, others wanted Crazy Horse to flee to Canada and join Sitting Bull. Crazy Horse took his wife to the Spotted Tail Agency.

Crazy Horse rode in with seven of his friends and some agency Indians to turn himself in at Fort Robinson, Nebraska, where he was about to be jailed on September 5, 1877.

The Chief wore a dark blue shirt, loin cloth, leggings and moccasins and one eagle feather in his glossy black hair; his red blanket was draped across his horse as he rode in to the fort.

Crazy Horse was told that he would not be harmed, but it was too late for talks that night and was led back to the "soldier house." In surprise Crazy Horse wrestled to escape jail. He pulled his knife, as Little-Big-Man grabbed him from behind. Crazy Horse yelled, "Let me go." He slashed Little-Big-Man's arm, but was stabbed in the back by the rifle bayonet of an Indian policeman, as he attempted to escape. The Sioux champion fell.

Touch-the-Clouds (photo, pg 138) and his father came to him at the guard house and remained with the dying Crazy Horse into the evening. Crazy Horse is quoted as to have said on his deathbed, "I shall be dead in a few minutes and will go to the Grandmother's country. I want you all to follow me."

In the night, life lapsed from the fallen warrior, as he mounted the great white stallion. He was buried in the Bighorns. In the words of the great Oglala Sioux Indian chief:

"My lands are where my dead be buried."

Crazy Horse

#47. Little-Big-Man
Courtesy of Azusa Publishing, L.L.C.

Chapter Seven
ESCAPE TO CANADA

Following the Battle of the Little Bighorn, some Lakota scattered into Canada, while others found refuge on other reservations. The Army pursued the Sioux people, and many surrendered to Colonel Nelson A. Miles and peacefully returned to their reservations. Others fled toward Canada, pursued by Colonel Miles' forces.

After the defeat of Custer and the 7th Cavalry at the Little Bighorn, Sitting Bull, a wanted man by the United States, would be hunted down and killed in America. He and his followers were not safe in their own country. Sitting Bull did not like the idea of giving up their lands and going onto reservations. Bear Coat was camped on the Tongue River and the pressure was on.

MacKenzie's troops sacked and burned the camp of Cheyenne Chief Dull Knife and Little Wolf, while Sitting Bull and his people endured the cold, harsh winter of 1876-1877. In 1876, most all of the Sioux Indians had been contained on reservations. Soldiers occupied the Dakota hunting grounds, leaving little to eat. The Indians had to contend with the cold as temperatures plummeted and the military could converge on their camp at any time, annihilate them, burn their teepees and shoot their horses. Unconditional surrender would cost them everything; they would be forced onto reservations. Sitting Bull's people were near starvation and their horses were gaunt, but he would not give in. He knew there was refuge in the Queen Mother's country.

There was no other choice but to fight on, as the Sioux would rather be killed in battle with honor than to suffer the humility of capture. Their options were few and life as they had known it was fleeting.

In the spring, Chief Sitting Bull began the long trek north from Montana. Sitting Bull counseled with the chiefs at Fort Peck. There was a skirmish there with Lt. Baldwin's company, before trading with the Slotas (French and Indian traders), who pulled oxcarts to haul their goods. He got enough ammunition to supply Crazy Horse, before pushing north across the chanku wakan (holy trail) or medicine line (international border) into Grandmother's country with 15 teepees of his Sioux. Canadian authorities watched their movement as they entered Canada.

The Sioux reached their destination in Canada early in 1877. Sitting Bull's party arrived at Jean Legare's trading post on Wood Mountain and sold furs for $30.00 cash. Sitting Bull and his band reached Pinto Horse Butte, and were confronted by James W. Walsh and a band of Canadian mounted Police. The Sioux rode out to meet them and they conferred on the edge of camp.

They met in a council lodge and talked. Twenty five Mounted Police detained the Canadian exiles. Using an interpreter, Major Walsh told Sitting Bull that they had sanctuary in Canada, but the Mounties would not tolerate horse theft in the Queen Mother's land or they would be punished and that the Royal Mounties would not tolerate them going on the war trail across the Holy Trail to raid in the United States from there, yet he welcomed them in Canada and told him to obey the laws of the Queen. In Canada, Sitting Bull befriended 34 year old Royal Mounted Police Major James Walsh, who played a huge role in his stay in the land of the Queen Mother.

Walsh knew the Sioux history and their fight for freedom and how the U.S. Army had driven them from their land. He also knew of the battle of the Little Bighorn and that they were fugitives seeking asylum. There was unrest in Canada. Fur trade companies ran illegal whiskey to the Indians. There was conflict between the tribes and strife between English and French fur traders.

Chief Sitting Bull had led his band over the Canadian prairie, but the buffalo populations were dwindling and food was scarce. The Sioux people were enduring hardships in Canada. Crazy Horse surrendered at Fort Robinson while Chief Sitting Bull was in Canada. There were 3,000 Sioux exiles in Canada in 1877.

An interesting anecdote is that at the tail end of the Nez Perce War in 1877, while General Miles was bartering peace with Chief Joseph in the Bear Paw Mountains, Nez Perce Chief White Bird and 103 men, 60 women and 8 children slipped away into Canada. The old chief escorted over one third of the non-treaty Nez Perce across the Bear Paw Mountains, into Canada.

By the spring of 1878, some 240 lodges of Crazy Horse's band arrived in Grandmother's country. Sitting Bull's village increased to 800 lodges, with White Bird's 45 Nez Perce lodges, totaling over 4,500 Sioux exiles in Canada. Some returned to Idaho over time, yet Nez Perce still reside in the foothills of the Canadian Rockies.

Bison were scarce in Canada, so Sitting Bull led his band of Sioux to the holy trail to hunt pte (buffalo) on the Milk River, July 17, 1879. The hunters moved farther north, as the women staked out buffalo skins to scrape the hides. Suddenly, two companies of Miles' Cavalry stormed the camp with 80 Cheyenne and Crow Indian scouts. The women scattered.

There were only 120 Dakota warriors present. Miles' Indian scouts tied red bandanas to their rifles, which confused the Sioux who thought it was a signal to parley. Instead, Miles' scouts initiated fire, killing two. Sioux warriors ran to help the women and children escape. Warriors rallied to fight them, but retreated when the Cavalry advanced.

A Crow warrior challenged Sitting Bull to a duel and he accepted, as the Crow scouts and the Sioux braves exchanged fire. Sitting Bull and Magpie faced each other and spurred their horses and rode hard to engage. Magpie's rifle misfired, as Sitting Bull took aim and fired, blowing off the top of Magpie's head; Sitting Bull claimed the scalp.

Many of the Sioux tribe left Canada and returned to the United States in 1879. Late in 1880, Sitting Bull and Gall had words; Gall took his band and crossed the Medicine Line and returned to America and surrendered at Standing Rock reservation, South Dakota, on January 3, 1881.

Gall moved onto the reservation and observed white man's ways. He took up farming and became a tribal judge. Gall told his friend, Indian Agent, James McLaughlin, that he was in love. He considered his wife at the time old, and desired another, who was already married. Gall told McLaughlin that he respected white man's law, but Indian law allowed him to steal her. However, he remained monogamous and did not pursue her.

Ten years after the Battle of the Little Bighorn, Gall returned to the Army, a fit 46 year old war chief and recounted Custer's Last Stand with dignity with feelings of sensitivity for the white man's loss. Gall was compared to General Hancock, a Civil War general. He was called the General Hancock of the Sioux.

Sitting Bull and his followers visited the Hudson's Bay post in the autumn of 1881, at Fort Qu'Appelle and asked the Indian Agent for food. They were turned down by the agency, which barely had enough food to feed the local Indians, and returned to Wood Mountain. Sitting Bull heard that Father Hugonard ordered a large quantity of flour the previous fall and approached him for some. Sitting Bull traded the priest a Navajo blanket for some flour.

Sitting Bull tried his hardest to get a reservation in Canada to house his people while he was there, to no avail. The chief wanted his people to be Canadians. His allegiance was to Canada, not America.

In 1881, Colonel MacLeod of the Royal Mounted Police, acted as an emissary to persuade Sitting Bull to return to the United States. MacLeod asked if there was a close friend to negotiate his position between Canada and the United States. Sitting Bull chose his friend, Jean Legare.

The story of the Battle of Little Bighorn was told to Legare by Sitting Bull, who relayed his own version to Fort Buford and the Canadian officials and made it sound better. He negotiated Sitting Bull's case to them. The authorities at Fort Buford asked Chief Sitting Bull to return to America. The chief then agreed to return.

Sitting Bull and the Hunkpapa band made the long trek back from Canada in 1881. The summer of 1881, Sitting Bull's party arrived at Fort Buford. On July 19, 1881, Sitting Bull and nine hundred eighty six of the Hunkpapa band surrendered at Fort Buford, North Dakota. Sitting Bull surrendered his Winchester carbine to the authorities. The Chief was then sent to Fort Randall and imprisoned for his war crimes, with no promised pardon.

#48. "Buffalo Bill"
William F. Cody
Courtesy of Azusa Publishing, L.L.C.

Chapter Eight
WILD WEST SHOW

William Fredrick Cody was born in Iowa, February 2, 1846. Cody moved to Kansas with his family and was only eleven when he left home to work as a drover herding cattle and also worked as a teamster. Cody went by the nickname Will. He traveled to Pike's Peak, Colorado for the famous Gold Rush there and later rode as one of 80 Pony Express Riders across America.

The Civil War broke out in 1861 and, when he turned eighteen, Will enlisted in February of 1864 with the 7th Kansas Regiment and served in the U.S. Army as a Union spy during the Civil War. Will penetrated Confederate lines by pretending to be a southern boy and reported General Forrest's position to Union Army General Smith. He also rode dispatch and as a hospital orderly in St. Louis, where he met his wife, Louisa Frederici in 1865.

After the war, he continued as a scout for the Army during the Indian Wars and became a famous frontier scout and Indian fighter. He met General William Tecumseh Sherman while a dispatch rider and became his scout. He guided Sherman to Bent's Fort and back. Will Cody ranked along with Daniel Boone and Kit Carson in popularity and was a great American hero.

After serving as a U.S. Army scout, Cody gained acclaim as a buffalo hunter. Cody reportedly shot over 4,000 buffalo to feed railroad employees and earned the nickname, "Buffalo Bill" Cody. He had a son, Kit Carson Cody and daughter. Will visited Denver and played opera houses in Central City and Georgetown. In 1871, Cody guided Gen. Sheridan, Gen. Custer and the Grand Duke of Russia on a buffalo hunt.

Just 26, in 1872, Cody went on the road with his stage play, "Scouts of the Prairie," a drama created by dime-novelist, Ned Buntline. Buntline developed Buffalo Bill's character into *Prince of the Plains* for his biography. He played Chicago with Texas Jack and Wild Bill Hickok. He played himself in Buntline's stage play "Buffalo Bill" in New York.

By 1875, Will wrote three books: *Deadly Eye, Prairie Prince, The Boy Outlaw* and *Scout* and *The Renegade*. Another novelist, Prentiss Ingraham wrote *Pony Express* and *Buffalo Bill's Frontier Feats.*

Buffalo Bill Cody co-owned a ranch near North Platte, Nebraska, called the Scouts Rest Ranch, where he resided. In 1882, the people of the community asked Cody to hold a rodeo in North Platte. Cody held his rodeo in on the Fourth of July and called it "the Old Glory Blowout," a first in America and performed his Wild West Show, there later. The next year he held his rodeo in Columbus, Nebraska. Cody was charitable, loved kids and gave tickets to orphanages.

The Wild West was based on actual historical events, races, rodeos, and sharpshooting. Buffalo Bill wanted to recreate the "Old West." Cody boasted of his feats, was a heavy drinker and a bit of a braggart. Regardless, he built a western show that appealed to the nation and was well loved. He used his poetic license to glorify himself playing out stories from his life.

Cody orchestrated a Wild West Show across America with hundreds of performers, agents and publicity people, under the big-top. Buffalo Bill hired American Indians from the beginning.

Will's press-agent was Major John W. Burke, who also went by Arizona John, was responsible for much of the success of the show.

Burke wore his hair past his shoulders and grew a flying buttress beard. He wore a Prince Albert Jacket and striped pants. Will's manager was Nate Salisbury. Burke had dime-novelists write semi-fictional books, supposedly by Buffalo Bill Cody. Bill later wrote an auto biography of the last forty years of his life.

Will Cody, tall, light haired and handsome, when dressed up in his western outfit and boots, he was quite the impressive figure. Buffalo Bill became quite the showman and brought the west to the people.

He was very famous and hob-knobbed with queens, princes and even President Cleveland. His show inspired nearly every red-blooded boy in America. Buffalo Bill's Original Wild West Show was deemed the most colossal spectacle on earth.

Born in 1860 of Quaker parents, Phoebe Anne Oakley Mozee became a marksman early. Annie hunted quail and rabbits on their farm and sold the game to the kitchen of the Cincinnati Hotel for their fine cuisine. Frank Butler, a promoter, came to Cincinnati with a shooting exhibition, using game birds as targets. Annie won the competition and married Frank Butler. The two took the shooting act on the road. In the spring of 1885, she signed with Buffalo Bill to perform in his show. Annie dropped the name, Phoebe and went by Annie Oakley to become famous in Buffalo Bill's Wild West Show.

Frank held a playing card in his hand; she could fire and slice it sideways or put a hole, dead-center at 30 paces with her rifle. Annie shot cartridges thrown in the air, exploding them. As her husband swung a ball around his head, Annie shot them over her shoulder, using a highly polished Bowie knife blade for a mirror. She peppered tin cans with her twin Colt revolvers. Annie was young and daring and the greatest shot in the world.

Gordon W. Lillie, later known as Pawnee Bill, was an interpreter at the Fort Sill Indian reservation. He borrowed Sioux Indians for his 1877-78 stage show, written by A.S. Burt, based on the Mountain Meadows Massacre, and involved Mormons and wild Indians ambushing a wagon train.

The Sioux Indian was a popular Plains tribe and became the model for the characterization of the American Indian. The Sioux appeared on the Indian head penny and the buffalo nickel. So Will Cody used Sioux Indians in his performances of the Wild West Show and made the Sioux famous.

Chief Sitting Bull made a number of public appearances and visited Bismarck, North Dakota to meet General Grant and headed a parade celebrating the opening of the Northern Pacific Railroad Transcontinental line.

Cody treated the Indians well. In the month of June in 1885, Buffalo Bill sent Major Burke to the reserve at the Standing Rock Agency to speak with Chief Sitting Bull, medicine man of the Sioux. He wanted the Chief to appear in his Wild West Show in the Indian Village.

Sitting Bull received permission to leave the reservation in 1885 to join the Wild West. Will made friends with Chief Sitting Bull. The Chief was devoted to Buffalo Bill, who he called *"Pahaska,"* (in the Sioux tongue, meaning Long Hair).

Cody wanted Gall and Chief Sitting Bull to appear as main attractions. Gall refused and said, "I am not an animal to be exhibited before the crowd."

Major Burke employed the Sioux and other Indians, and first offered them a cigar, before promising a whole box of cigars. Buffalo Bill held him to his promise. He said that he should not break that promise or he would never be any good to him on the show.

#49. Buffalo Bill's Wild West Show
North Platte, Nebraska
Courtesy of Azusa Publishing, L.L.C.

#50. Annie Oakley, World's Greatest Shot
Buffalo Bill's Wild West Show
Courtesy of Azusa Publishing, L.L.C.

#51. "Wild Bill Hickok"
Courtesy of Azusa Publishing, L.L.C.

#52. Sitting Bull & Buffalo Bill in Wild West
Courtesy of Azusa Publishing, L.L.C.

#53. "Buffalo Bill"
Courtesy of Azusa Publishing Company, L.L.C.

Major Burke made Sitting Bull a proposal to tour with the Wild West for the sum of fifty dollars a week, plus expenses. As Burke wrote the terms of the contract, Sitting Bull demanded one more concession; he wanted sole rights to sell his photographs and of visitors posing with him by tintype concessionaire. Sitting Bull signed the contract.

Sitting Bull joined the Wild West at Buffalo, New York and was a big hit with the fans. They played in many major American cities and Canada. The chief sold hundreds of photographs to them. Major Burke told the newspapers, when Sitting Bull joined the show that he had adopted Annie Oakley (photo, pg 154) as his daughter, "*Watanya Cicilia*," in Sioux meant, "Little Sure Shot."

The Sioux word, "*oskate wicasa*" (show man) described their role as performers in the Wild West Show were called "show Indians." Will also used Arapaho, Cheyenne and Pawnee Indians in his Wild West Show. Other famous Indians were Chief Joseph and Apache Chief Geronimo.

They reenacted actual U.S. Army and Indian battles with the U.S. Army, like the Little Bighorn, Wounded Knee and also the Ghost Dance. Will played roles with the Indians. In his show were Texas Jack, Pawnee Bill and Wild Bill Hickok (photo, pg. 155), his oldest friend. He brought the frontier to the people.

During the Wild West Show, Chief Sitting Bull became the main attraction and sat with dignity on his horse. Because of Custer's Last Stand some of the spectators booed the chief, but he persevered and did not complain and no problems arose over it.

Buffalo Bill defended Sitting Bull and the Sioux, saying that the Little Bighorn was not a massacre and that the 7th U.S. Cavalry fought with orders to kill Indians, who fought to protect their families and lands from the white man. He said Sitting Bull did not lead the assault against Custer, that Crazy Horse and Gall were the war chiefs, who killed Custer.

Many of his cast was Sioux Indians, like American Horse, Flying Horse, Has-No-Horse, High Heron, Kicking Bear, Kills First, No Neck, Rain-In-the-Face, Red Cloud, Red Shirt, Rocky Bear, Samuel Lone Bear, Sitting Bull, Short Bull, Short Man, Spotted Tail, Two Bulls, Two Lance, Two Strike, Young-Man-Afraid-of-His-Horses, and Willie Spotted Horse.

Red Cloud and Sitting Bull were most famous. Newspaper coverage of events of the two chiefs had become made them folk heroes. American Horse was a peacemaker of his tribe in Washington and later was in the show.

The Wild West Show received good newspaper coverage and called Annie Oakley, Little Missy and raved about her shooting. The press did a good job of covering Sitting Bull, also. Canadian fans received the Wild West Show with open arms and had no ill feelings about Chief Sitting Bull and the Little Bighorn.

The 1885 season ended in St. Louis after more than a million dollar gross that year. Sitting Bull terminated his contract, after touring the show for just one year, in 1885. When Sitting Bull left the show, Buffalo Bill gifted him a beautiful prize stallion. Buffalo Bill had wanted the chief to go on the grand tour to Europe in 1887, but it was not possible for him to participate.

When Buffalo Bill traveled to London, England, with the Wild West Show in 1885, they appeared at Earl's Court in London, attended by Lady Randolph Churchill, Sir Charles Wyndham , Gilbert & Sullivan, the Prince of Wales (Edward the VII), the princess, and their three daughters.

Edward sent a note to Buffalo Bill, calling him Sir Will, requesting a friendly shooting match the following day at 10:30, between Annie and the Grand Duke Michael of Russia, who was in Europe to marry.

She beat the Duke miserably in every match. He was mortified when his intended broke off the engagement after he was beaten by a woman. The Prince of Whales, who had seen the show many times, presented her with a medal.

Queen Victoria commanded an audience with Annie Oakley and was delighted with her performance. Black Elk, an Oglala Sioux, called Queen Victoria "Grandmother England." Other members of the troupe were feeling ignored. Annie caused such a stir with royalty that seemed to steal the thunder from the Wild West Show. Had Annie Oakley gotten too big for her britches?

When it came time to board ship, Mr. and Mrs. Butler did not show. Instead they went to Berlin and toured Germany. The ship sailed for America, without them. After the tour of Germany, they returned to America.

Annie joined the Deadwood Dick stage show before touring vaudeville. The troupe left New York to cross the Atlantic March 31, 1887, on the steamship, the State of Nebraska. The entourage included 83 saloon passengers, 138 steerage passengers, 97 Indians, 18 buffaloes, two deer, ten elk, 10 mules, 5 Texas steers, four donkeys and 108 horses. They performed for the Queen.

In 1889, Annie and Frank returned to the Wild West. The Show returned to Europe in 1889-1890 and toured England, France, Germany and Spain. In Berlin, Annie shot the ashes of the cigarette in the mouth of the Kaiser Wilhelm. In 1901, she was the sensation at the Chicago World's Fair.

The next seven years, Annie performed in the Wild West. That year, the train carrying the show was bound for the winter quarters in the south collided with another train head-on. Four performers were killed and 100 wounded.

Annie Oakley was pulled from the train, unconscious and partially paralyzed and in need of five operations. Her hair turned white. For two years, Annie convalesced, but she could still shoot.

She first appeared on vaudeville and taught shooting. Annie passed away in Greenville, Ohio on November 3, 1926; Frank followed her in passing a few weeks later.

In 1913, Buffalo Bill's Wild West Show wound down in Denver, when outstanding debts closed the show down. Heavily in debt to Denver businessman Harry Tammen, Cody was forced to appear in the Tammen-Sells-Floto-Circus to pay off his debt and the show was sold at auction.

Four years later, Buffalo Bill Cody died in 1917. It was his preference that he be buried atop Lookout Mountain in Colorado. His wife, Louisa was interred beside him in 1921.

Buffalo Bill was a legendary figure and performer around the world. Cody, Wyoming, the home of the Buffalo Bill Museum was named after him. Millions have visited his grave. "Buffalo Bill" Cody's death was the end of a historic legend.

Buffalo Bill was a scout, express rider, buffalo hunter, author, actor and showman. He brought joy to the young and old alike through his wild West Show. Buffalo Bill's rodeo caught on and was the forerunner to the modern rodeos of today.

#54. Burial Pyre
Courtesy of Azusa Publishing, L.L.C.

Chapter Nine
GHOST DANCE

Sioux story tellers told tales of ghostly apparitions that put fear in the hearts of the Indians. Most American Indians believed in ghosts and feared them. The Sioux were superstitious of unknown mythical creatures.

They believed that illness was a demon entering the human body. The medicine man sometimes feigned to suck the evil spirit out of the person's body. Deer claw rattles, eagle bone whistles and drums were used, accompanied by the Shaman's chanting, incantations and prayers to cure.

Indians avoided entering a sacred burial ground. The Sioux waited twenty four hours before burial of the dead to make sure that the person was actually dead. The family assisted in the preparation of the body.

When a Sioux warrior died, he was wrapped in the skin of a newly killed buffalo that was still moist. Rawhide thongs were tied around the corpse to seal it from exposure to the air. The body was tied to a travois behind a horse and carried in a grand parade to the site of the burial.

The most common type of burial was the platform type. A scaffold was constructed of four willow sapling uprights, about seven feet in the air, to deter predators, with branches tied across to support the body, with the head facing the rising sun (god). Other tribes, like the Shoshoni, used subterranean burials in crevices, covered with rocks.

During the winter, trees were sometimes used to replace the scaffold if the ground was frozen. Tree burials were regularly practiced by Northern tribes. A tree fork, formed of large branches, supported the body in the air.

All of the warrior's possessions were placed beside him: bow and arrows, pipe and tobacco bag and fire making tools. Enough food for his long journey to the spiritual world was laid beside him, while his war shield and lance, medicine bag, and a horse tail hung over him. His favorite horse was shot, painted with red war paint for the hereafter, and placed near the body.

A loved one would slash across his/her limbs to mutilate the body in mourning and begin to wail or chant. One drastic practice of the Sioux if a loved one died was to amputate their finger as a sign of mourning.

Spirits of dead enemies they had scalped cast fear into these Indians. They believed that souls of the dead Indians could come to life to haunt them. Some Plains Indians believed the souls of dead warriors entered the bodies of large, black, blue and white scavenger birds called magpies. To hear the birds' mournful call could remind a person of a distant warrior's war cry.

In 1872, Smohalla, a Nez Perce prophet, said that Indians would rise from the dead to drive the white-eyes out, initiating the Dreamer's Religion.

Ogallala Sioux Chief American Horse was a diplomat to the government for his people. After the Wounded Knee Uprising, he became the leader of the Sioux delegation to Washington. In 1877, a Sioux delegation visited Washington for talks with President Rutherford B. Hayes in 1877.

The Sioux Indians had been embattled by the U.S. Army for decades to defend their homeland and after the Battle of the Little Bighorn were beaten and destined to live out their lives on reservations.

Reservation life was supposed to settle and make them civilized. Instead, it had taken away the Indians' lands, horses, buffalo and beaver, even their firearms.

In 1880, 16,000 Teton Sioux dwelled on the Great Sioux Reservation at Rosebud, South Dakota. The reservation was bounded on the east by the Missouri River, on the west by the periphery of the Black Hills and on the north by the Cannonball River and on the south by the Nebraska line.

On August 5, 1881, Sioux warrior Crow Dog shot and killed Spotted Tail, a member of his tribe. Crow Dog's family paid restitution of $600.00, eight horses and one blanket to the family of Spotted Tail. March 3, 1885, the U.S. Congress passed the Major Crimes Act, in response to the 1883 Ex Parte Crow Dog decision by the Supreme Court.

In 1885, Indian police were established on 48 of 60 Indian reservations. February 8, 1887, the Dawes Allotment Act was passed by the United States to break up communally owned Indian land and allotted 160 acre parcels to Indian families. It also authorized the government to cede surplus Indian lands to the white settlers, adding to the Indians' misery. The objective of the act was to move the Indians into American society. They were left in despair and desolation. When word of the Ghost Dance came, it gave them hope to gain their lands back and to drive the white man from their land.

The Sioux Act of 1889 broke the Great Sioux Reservation down into six smaller reservations. In 1889, Kicking Bear painted his detailed pictograph rendition of the scene after Custer's last stand on a deerskin for the famous western artist, Fredrick Remington, when he visited Montana.

Charles Eastman, a Dakota Sioux student graduated from Dartsmouth, earned a medical degree from Boston University in 1889. That year, an Omaha Sioux, Susan La Flesche became the first female Indian doctor.

Wavoca, a Paiute holy man in Nevada, called Jack Wilson, taught by Christian missionaries to observe the golden rule came to be called "the messiah."

On January 1, 1889, Wavoca had a vision of immortal warriors in painted deerskin war shirts (Ghost shirts) dancing in a circle, invincible to white man's bullets in the "Ghost Shirt Religion." Some white men called it the "Indian Messiah Movement."

The American Indian population in America was just under 250,000 people in 1890. The Ghost Dance excitement spread from Nevada to Fort Hall and on to the Plains, reaching the Sioux by 1890. Kicking Bear was a leader of the Ghost Dance movement, a thing of sanctity, who found a connection between the Ghost Dance and their creator god.

Many Sioux braves believed the myth of the Ghost Shirt Dance and the U. S. Army feared rebellion resulting from their performing the Ghost Dance. The frenzy spread to hundreds of Indians to rally and fight the white man with hope of redemption. Brule Chief Crow Dog was active in the Ghost Shirt Movement and was known for killing Brule Chief Spotted Tail. Sitting Bull was told of the Ghost Dance by Kicking Bear and did not take much stock in it. Sitting Bull and Big Foot were listed as hostiles.

The Indians spread rumors that Chief Sitting Bull, being a medicine man, was going to raise all of the Indians from the dead and they were going to run the white man out of Indian country. Chief Red Cloud opposed the Ghost Dance and instead acted as a peace chief, but could not control the young braves. Red Cloud knew the white man's strength. Young Sioux braves did the Ghost Dance on December 14, 1890, in their sacred shirts, late in the night giving war-whoops, shooting off rifles, and dancing around a huge bonfire at Wounded Knee frightening nearby settlers.

The original order from the Bureau of Indian Affairs was passed on to the Akicita (Indian police) Chief Bull Head was to arrest Sitting Bull and bring him in to custody on December 15, 1890. Instead, forty three Lakota policemen were sent to apprehend him. The numbers were too great.

The Battle on the Grand River occurred when the Indian police came to Sitting Bull's cabin to arrest him and charge him with being responsible for the Ghost Dance of the previous night. Early in the morning, the next day, the Indian police broke down the door of Chief Sitting Bull's cabin at Standing Rock Reservation at Wounded Knee, South Dakota. Sergeant Red Tomahawk interpreted that order, as to deliver his corpse to the agent. There were ill feelings between the Akicitia and Hunkpapa Indians. The Hunkpapa people jeered the police saying that they would not take Chief Sitting Bull.

Bull Head and Sitting Bull had been rivals. There was animosity and jealousy between some chiefs and other Indians. The Indian police arrived and a fire fight began. A bullet pierced Bull Head's side; he shot Sitting Bull in the chest, killing him. It was an assassination, not an arrest.

Some of Sitting Bull's warriors returned fire; five of his friends were killed: Black Bird, Spotted Horn Bull, Brave Thunder, his brother Jumping Bull and his son and several of the Akicita lay dead. Tragically, Sioux Chief Sitting Bull was killed by Indian police as an example to others. Bull Head died that day, too. The ambulance arrived, but there was discord over both the Akicitia and the Hunkpapa dead being transported in the same vehicle.

Sioux Chief Sitting Bull was probably the most or one of the most famous American Indians of all time. Sitting Bull's death was the passing of an era. And so it was, the great chiefs, Crazy Horse and Sitting Bull had died violent deaths, needlessly at the hands of their own people.

After the chief's death, the Hunkpapa people from Sitting Bull's camp fled to the Cheyenne River reservation to the south and joined Chief Big Foot's band at Cherry Creek, South Dakota. They journeyed from there to the Pine Ridge reservation under Chief Red Cloud. The Sioux prepared to go to war, but Chief American Horse convinced them to go along with the treaty.

Alarmed after the Ghost Dance, officials banned the Ghost Dance on reservations in December of 1890, but the dance continued and troops were called to Pine Ridge. The Army, led by General Nelson A. Miles, readied for more fighting. Many Indian tribes surrendered to Miles in his 1876-1877 Campaign, but the Brule and Oglala Sioux at Pine Ridge resisted.

General "Bear Coat" Miles ordered Major Whitside and the 7th Cavalry to round up Bigfoot and his band and to arrest Chief Big Foot, who dwelled along the Cheyenne River in South Dakota, but he had already left with his people for Pine Ridge on Red Cloud's invitation to insure peace.

They searched the Badlands and found the Minneconjou camped on Porcupine Creek, 30 miles east of Pine Ridge reservation. They put up no resistance. Chief Big Foot was sick with pneumonia and had to be transported by Army wagon. The Sioux were ordered to set up camp at Wounded Knee Creek, five miles to the west. Colonel James Forsyth took command and ordered the soldiers to place four Hotchkiss cannons around the Indian's camp.

The military numbered 500 strong, while the Chief Big Foot's Minneconjou Sioux people, including some Hunkpapa, totaled 350, while two thirds of those were women and children. Instead of providing them an escort, Forsyth's command demanded the Indians relinquish their weapons and confiscated them.

On December 29, 1890, 500 7th Cavalry and Buffalo Soldiers arrived at Wounded Knee in South Dakota Territory with orders to escort the Indians to the railroad for transport to Omaha, Nebraska. The 7th, armed with four rapid-fire (Hotchkiss guns), stormed the encampment of the Lakota Sioux Indians, to ambush the Sioux, because of the Ghost Dance incident.

A medicine man named Yellow Bird told the Sioux to resist and said that their Ghost Shirts would protect them. As the drama unfolded, a soldier tried to wrest a rifle from a deaf Indian, named Black Coyote; it discharged and shots rang out, as soldiers fought the Sioux hand-to-hand.

The Indians literally ran for their lives, but the military directed cannon fire at them, killing men, women and children, and left their bodies lying in the snow. Less than an hour later, 150 Indians had needlessly died, with 50 wounded. It was no less than genocide. Twenty five soldiers were killed and thirty nine wounded.

Nearly 150 Sioux Indians fled from camp that day and ran into the wintery snow and cold; some died of hypothermia. Many reached the Cheyenne River Reservation; some escaped to Chief Big Foot's Cherry Creek Agency, while others fled into Canada. Big Foot surrendered to the Army.

The Medicine Man's dream had become a nightmare as the U.S. Military killed hundreds of unarmed Sioux Indian men, women and children in the Battle of Wounded Knee, South Dakota. Many warriors fought to the death, in order to keep from being taken prisoner and disgrace the Sioux name.

The troops' presence made things worse. Short Bull and Kicking Bear brought their tribes people northwest corner of the Pine Ridge Reserve. The dancers sent word to Sitting Bull and the Hunkpapa to join them, but before he could act, Sitting Bull had been assassinated.

On January 15, 1891, U.S. Army troops marched to the wintery scene of the Wounded Knee Massacre and collected the contorted frozen remains of the victims and buried them in a mass grave.

The massacre was the last major conflict between the Lakota and the United States. Forsyth was later charged with the massacre, but was exonerated.

After Wounded Knee, Kicking Bear led a band of about 2,700 Lakota, less than half were warriors, in the last Sioux uprising and was on the war trail 18 days attacking Army columns and posts. Kicking Bear and his band struggled during the cold Dakota winter of 1891. In 1892, 400 Brule and Oglala Sioux Indians banded together on the Brule River at the "Great Hostile Camp," near Pine Ridge.

War seemed imminent, but a treaty was signed with General Miles. They returned to the agency January 15, 1891. Kicking Bear laid his rifle at Bear Coat's feet and ended the Ghost Dance War, forever. American Horse went to Washington and obtained rations and better treatment of his people.

January 7, 1891, over the Wounded Knee Massacre, a Lakota Indian, Plenty Horses killed an Army Lieutenant Edward Casey on Pine Ridge Reservation.

Chapter Ten
RESERVATIONS

The era of the Indian Wars had passed. Peace finally came, but at what price? Indian populations had been greatly decreased from white man's liquor, disease and the loss of the beaver and buffalo, and thousands of lives. In the late 1800's Indians were forced to live on Indian reservations. The change from living on the Plains to reservation life caused the Indians oppression. They suffered starvation, disease, and poverty on reservations.

Despite giving up their culture as they knew it, the American Indians have fared rather well. The "Vanishing American," as the Indian was once portrayed, is very much alive on the horizon and definitely not going away. Although the Indians have had their trials and dysfunction, as most American families have had, they have a bright future today.

The Assiniboine and Yanktonai reunited at the Fort Peck Indian reservation in Montana, where they reside. They allied and hunted buffalo with the Yantonai Sioux in northern Montana. The Assiniboine also joined the River Crow and Gros Ventre and lodged near Fort Belknap and were careful to avoid the fierce Blackfeet. In 1869, the Gros Ventre and Assiniboine tribes suffered another smallpox epidemic and the buffalo were rapidly disappearing. The Lower Assiniboine led by Chief Red Stone that lived on the lower Missouri, were not affected by the plague. The Fort Peck Agency was established in 1871 around them.

By November 26, 1884, the Tongue River Reservation was established. In 1900, the boundaries were expanded to its present size. Over time, the Northern Cheyenne was supported by farming and timber. Their land was retained and was not allotted to settlers. The government tried to introduce enemy Crow Indians onto their reservation, to no avail. Today, ninety per cent of the original reservation is tribal owned.

March 2, 1889, the Lakota Sioux sold 9 million acres in the western Dakotas to the U.S., which broke the Great Sioux reservation into smaller reserves.

By 1890, the population at Fort Peck was a little more than 1,000 Yanktonai, over 700 Lower Missouri Assiniboine and other Sioux bands.

Smithsonian Institute curators made a plaster cast of Iron Elk, an Oglala Indian warrior from the Pine Ridge Agency in the early 1900's. Chief Gall died at his home in Oak Creek, South Dakota on December 5, 1894.

In March of 1896, Kicking Bear and two other Sioux chieftains took their grievances to Washington D. C. to the Bureau of Indian Affairs. While in Washington, Kicking Bear agreed to have a life mask made as the face of the "Sioux Warrior" to be displayed in the Smithsonian Institute of Natural History adorned with his own buckskin shirt and leggings, and tobacco pouch.

On June 28, 1898, the U.S. Congress passed the Curtis Act, which extended allotments to Indian Territory and abolished Indian jurisdiction.

In 1899, the buffalo population dropped from several million to place them as an endangered species.

Red Cloud converted to Catholicism. He lived in the house that the U.S. government had built until he died at Pine Ridge, December 9, 1909.

In 1910, a Winnebago man, named Henry Red Cloud earned his B.A. degree from Yale University.

On April 6, 1917, 12,000 American Indians volunteered to serve in W.W.I, in the armed forces. In 1919, the U.S. government granted citizenship to all American Indian veterans of W.W.I.

Plenty Horses, who killed Spotted Tail, died in 1933.

The Indian Reorganization Act of 1934 ended the allotment of all tribal lands and attempted to recover the surplus lands that have not been homesteaded. Also in 1934, Congress passed the Johnson-O'Malley Act to provide more money to local school districts that accept and educate Indian students. May 1, 1936, Congress extended the Reorganization Act to Alaska.

The U.S. government required American Indians in the U.S. to register for the military, yet they were not allowed to vote. In 1942, the U.S. Marines developed a Navajo Code Talker Unit of 400 Navajos, who served in the Pacific. A similar Comanche Code Talker Unit was also developed.

From 1939-1945, Twenty five thousand American Indians served in the armed forces during World War II and 40,000 American Indians left home to take war-related jobs.

Tribal enrollment at Fort Peck is controlled by the 1960 Tribal Ordinance, which maintains that tribal members before 1960 must be on the tribal roles and be approved by the Secretary of the Interior. Members enrolled since 1960 must have one quarter Assiniboine or Sioux blood.

In 1973, the Oglala Sioux Indians staged an armed occupation of the Wounded Knee Community. Today, the Oglala Sioux Nation still lives on.

They are a proud people, not to be beaten down and forgotten. Some are doctors, lawyers and businessmen and women. The Lakota Sioux Indians are a strong, courageous Nation today.

Today, the Sioux Indians maintain many reservations with their own tribal governments. Half of enrolled members live off the reserves. There are 24 Sioux reserves in Minnesota, Montana, Nebraska, North Dakota, and South Dakota in America. Canadian reserves are in Manitoba and Saskatchewan.

The majority of Sioux Reservations in the United States are in South Dakota. The ones listed below are in South Dakota. The Blackfoot, Minneconjou, San Arc Sioux and Two Kettle Sioux Indians dwell on the Cheyenne River Indian Reservation. The Crow Creek Indian Reservation of Blackfoot, Minneconjou, Sans Arc, and the Two Kettle Sioux are made up of the Yanktonai Sioux.

The Flandreau Santee Indian Reserve is composed of Mdewakanton, Wahpekute and Wahpeton bands of Sioux Indians. The Lake Traverse Indian Reservation takes in the Sisseton and Wahpeton Sioux tribes. The Lower Brule Indian Reservation is made up of the Lower Brule Sioux Indian tribe. The Pine Ridge Indian Reservation is composed of the Yankton Sioux Indians. On the Rosebud Indian reservation dwell the Sicangu Brule Sioux and some Oglalas. The Spirit Lake Indian Reservation consists of the Sisseton, Upper Yanktonai, and Wahpeton tribes. The Yankton Sioux dwell on the Yankton Sioux Indian Reservation. The above reservations are solely in South Dakota.

The Standing Rock Indian Reservation is in North Dakota and South Dakota, that being . The Hunkpapa and Upper Yanktonia lodge there.

One Sioux Indian reserve is in Montana, the Fort Peck Indian Reservation contains the Hunkpapa, Mdewakantonwan, Sisseton, Wahpekute, Wahpeton and the Canoe Paddler and Red Bottom Assiniboine Indians. In 1990, there were 10,595 lodged on the reservation, but only 5,782 were Indians. Fort Peck in 1993 had 10,693 enrolled members that lived primarily near the southern boundary. Five thousand three hundred twelve lived off the reservation. Fort Peck has grown rapidly the last twenty years and the Indian population has increased 82%, with a decreasing non-Indian population. Reservation lands make up 2,093,318 acres, more than 56% is non-Indian owned. As of 1993, Indian members own 508,412 acres. The tribes own 396,124 acres; much is agricultural, grazing, and irrigated crops.

Minnesota has four Sioux reservations: the Upper Reservation where the Mdewakanton, Sisseton and Wahpeton Sioux Indians lodge; the Lower Sioux Indian Reservation where the Mdewakanton and Wahpekute Sioux lodge in Minnesota; the Shakopee-Mdewakanton Indian Reservation, also in Minnesota; and the Prairie Island Indian Community, made up of Mdewakanton and Wahpekute Sioux Indians.

The Santee Indian Reservation is in Nebraska and consists of the Mdewakanton Sioux and the Wahpekute Sioux Indians.

There are five Sioux Indian Reservations in Manitoba, Canada. The Sioux Valley Dakota Nation Reserve and Fishing Station Reserve is where the Sisseton, Mdewakanton, Wahpeton and Wahpekute Sioux Indians dwell.

The Wahpeton and Sisseton Sioux reside at the Dakota Plains Indian Reserve. Another reserve in Manitoba is called the Dakota Tipi 1 Reserve. The people there are Wahpeton Sioux Indians. The Bird Tail Creek 57 Reserve, Bird Tail Hay Lands 57A Reserve and Fishing Station 62A Reserve, the Mdewakanton, Wahpeton and Yanktonai Sioux lodge there. The Canupawakpa Dakota First Nation Reserve, Oak Lake 59A Reserve, Fishing Station 62A Reserve, the Wahpekute, Wahpeton and Yanktonai Sioux all dwell in Manitoba.

Saskatchewan has four Sioux Indian Nation Reserves. The Standing Buffalo 78 Reserve people are the Sisseton and Wahpeton Sioux. Whitecap Reserve in Saskatchewan has Sisseton and Wahpeton Sioux residing there. Dakota Plains Nation of Saskatchewan, Canada is a reserve of Wahpeton Sioux Indians. Wood Mountain 160 Reserve, Treaty Four Reserve Grounds Indian Reservation, 77 in Saskatchewan is made up of Hunkpapa Sioux.

The Indian population in America in 2000 was 2,475,950. Some tribes became extinct by 1900, but others have prospered and grown. Canada boasts 160,000 Indian residents, Alaska 37,000 Eskimos, Aleuts and Indians.

Sioux Indian reservations retain their culture. The tribes are a tight knit organization with the tribal council and their own government. They have fairs, powwows and rodeos. During celebrations they tell stories, sing and hold dances, like the old days. Festivities involve feasting and much festivity.

Education is emphasized and colleges are turning out much needed Indian doctors, lawyers and nurses. Many Indians live off of the reservation, also. There are many successful Sioux ranchers and businessmen, today. The Sioux Nation owns the Dakota Magic Casino & Hotel in Hankinson, North Dakota and the Dakota Sioux Casino & Hotel in Watertown, South Dakota.

Demographics for Native Americans in the United States numbered 250,000 in the year 1900 and by 1960, the American Indian population was 524,000, according to records kept by the Indian tribes and the Bureau of Indian Affairs. The total Indian population in the United States in 2005 was 4.5 million. The U.S. Census in 2010 of the Sioux Indian population reached 131,048. The Cheyenne Indian population in 2010 was 11,688. The American Indian and Alaskan Native population in 2010 was 2,932,248.

INDEX

179

Bibliography

Andrews, Elaine, *Indians of the Plains*, Benford Books, Inc., New York, 1992.

Axelrod, Alan, *Chronicles of the Indian Wars*, Prentice Hall, New York, 1993.

Bryant Jr., William L.,*Montana's Indians, Yesterday and Today,* American & World
Publishers, Helena, 1996.

Convis, Charles L., *Native American Women*, Pioneer Press, Carson City, 1996.

Convis, Charles L., *Warriors & Chiefs of the West*, Pioneer Press, Carson City, 1994.

Garst, Shannon, Sitting Bull, *Champion of his People,* Julian Messner,
New York, 1970.

Grant, Bruce, *Concise Encyclopedia of the American Indian*, Wings Books,
New York, 1989

Hoebel, E. Adamson, *The Cheyennes*, Holt, Rinehart and Winston, New York, 1960.

Mails, Thomas E., *The Mystic Warriors of the Plain*s, Mallard Press, New York, 1991.

O'Neal, Bill, *Best of the West,* Lincolnwood, Illinois, Publications Intl., Ltd., 2006.

O'Reilly, Bill & Dugard, Martin, *Killing Lincoln*, Henry Holt & Company, L.L.C.,
New York, 2011

Sell, Henry Blackman and Weybright, Victor, Buffalo *Bill and the West*,
New York, Oxford University Press, 1955.

The Editors, *The Mighty Chieftains*, Time-Life Books, Alexandria, Virginia, 1993.

Utley, Robert M., *The Lance and the Shield,* Henry Holt & Company,
New York, 1993.

Utley, Robert M. & Washburn, E., *The American Heritage History of the Indian
Wars*, Simon & Schuster, Inc., New York, 1929.

Wyman, Walker D., *The Wild Horse of the Wes*t, Caxton Printers, Ltd., Caldwell,
Idaho, 1945.

Citing Electronic Publications

<http://www.angelfire.com/wy/9infantry/battle3.html>
<http://www.answers.com/topic/dull-knife_campaign>
<http://www.bgsu.edu/departments/acs/1890s/buffalobill/
bbwildwestshow.html>

<http://www.buffalobill.com/BuffaloBill.02.html>
<http://www.buffalobill.org/History%20Research%20on%20the
%20Buffalo%20Bill%20html>

<http://www.buffalosolddier.net/>
<http://www.custerlives.com/indians11.htm>
<http://www.dlncoalition.org/dln_nation/chief_gall.htm>
<http://www.enotes.com/topic/Battle_of_Cedar_creek_ (1876)>
<http://www.en.wikipedia.org/wiki/Sioux>
<http://www.factmonster.com/ipka/A0762159.html>
<http://www.kstrom.net/isk/arvol/buffpipe.html>
<http://www.lifeinitiativesinc.org/lakota.html>
<http://www.legendsofamerica.com/na-indianwarbattles-2.html>
<http://www.legendsofamerica.com/na-timeline3.html>
<http://www.legendsofamerica.com/na-timeline4.html>
<http://www.legendsofamerica.com/na-timeline5html>
<http://www.mysteriesof.com/Saskatchewan/sitting_bull.htm>canada
<http://www.native-languages.org/famsio.htm>
<http://www.nps.gov/hps/abpp/battles/nd001.htm>
<http://www.nps.gov/history/history/outline_books/fola/mattes/chap1.htm>
<http://www.olden-times.com/oldtimenebraska/n-csnyder/nbstory/
story19.html>

<http://www.pbs.org/weta/thewest/people/i_r/redcloud.htm>
<http://www.segonku.unl.edu/~jheppler/showindian//analysis/show-
indians/>

<http://www.snowowl.com/peoplecomanche.html>
<http://www.snowowl.com/peoplesioux.html>
<http://www.visitmt.com/history/Montana_the_Magazine_of_Western_
History/wolfMountain .htm>

The author explores inside 19th Century stone house in southeastern Oregon.

About the Author

Born in Lexington, Nebraska, Robert Bolen, B.A. has a degree in Archeology/ Anthropology. In Archeology class he was informed that, because of his features, the Mongolian Eye-fold, that he was part Indian. In 1755, a Bolen ancestor was taken captive by Delaware Indians. She was later rescued with her baby daughter, Robb's great, great, grandmother. At the time of rescue, the poor girl (just 17) was scalped, but lived. The French scalp was the size of a silver dollar. Family says that she combed her hair hiding the scar and managed to live to be over one hundred years of age. Bolens served under George Washington in the American Revolution. In 1777, the author's ancestors erected Fort "Bolin" near Cross Creek, Pennsylvania for protection from Indian attacks. Two ancestors were killed in Kentucky by Shawnee Indians allied to the British. Great Granddad Gilbert Bolen rode with the Ohio Fourth Cavalry in the Civil War under General Sherman. In 1866, he brought his wife and six children west to Nebraska in a Conestoga wagon. Granddad Denver Colorado Bolen knew Buffalo Bill Cody in western Nebraska.

Bolen is an authority on Indian artifacts and trade beads. Robb and Dori Bolen reside in Nampa, near Boise, Idaho. Robb owns the website, Fort Boise Bead Trader.com.

PHOTOGRAPHS
COURTESY
OF

AZUSA Publishing, LLC
3575 S. Fox Street
Englewood, CO 80110

Email: azusa@azusapublishing.com
Phone Toll-free: 888-783-0077
Phone/Fax: 303-783-0073

Mailing address:
AZUSA Publishing, LLC
P.O. Box 2526
Englewood, Co. 89150

CPSIA information can be obtained
at www.ICGtesting.com
Printed in the USA
FFHW022129230819
54372757-60121FF

9 781450 795203